KU-469-450

THE TRAVAILS OF
SANCHO PANZA

QUEEN MARGARET COLLEGE LIBRARY

JAMES SAUNDERS

THE TRAVAILS OF
SANCHO PANZA

A Play for the Young

HEINEMANN

Heinemann Educational Books Ltd
LONDON EDINBURGH MELBOURNE TORONTO
SINGAPORE JOHANNESBURG AUCKLAND
IBADAN HONG KONG NAIROBI

SBN 435 23787 x (cased)
SBN 435 23788 8 (paperback)

© James Saunders 1970
First published 1970

**All rights whatsoever in this play are strictly
reserved and application for performance etc.
should be made before rehearsal to Margaret
Ramsey Ltd. 14a Goodwin's Court, London
W.C.2. No performance may be given unless a
licence has been obtained**

Published by
Heinemann Educational Books Ltd,
48 Charles Street, London WIX 8AH
Printed in Great Britain by
Cox & Wyman Ltd,
London, Fakenham and Reading

CHARACTERS

Don Quixote's HOUSEKEEPER
his NIECE
a STUDENT
a PRIEST
NICHOLAS, a barber
DON QUIXOTE
SANCHO PANZA
MARIA, a servant at the Inn
an INNKEEPER
a CARRIER
an OFFICER of the Holy Brotherhood
a shepherd LAD
a FARMER, his master
a Benedictine MONK
his SERVANT
a PIGMAN
a travelling BARBER
BANDITS, TRAVELLERS, MONKS, etc.

SCENES

ONE: *The courtyard of Don Quixote's house*
TWO: *The road*
THREE: *The stableyard of the Inn*
FOUR: *The loft of the Inn*
FIVE: *As Scene Three*
SIX: *The road*
SEVEN: *As Scene One*
EIGHT: *The road*
NINE: *As Scene Three*
TEN: *The desert*
ELEVEN: *As Scene Three*
TWELVE: *As Scene One*

SCENE ONE

The courtyard of the house of Senor Quixada, or DON QUIXOTE
as he will be called, with the house behind it.

From a window come noises as if a battle were going on: thumps,
bangs, and the sound of DON QUIXOTE'S *voice. In the courtyard*
his HOUSEKEEPER, *his* NIECE *and the* STUDENT, *books under*
his arm, are listening to the rumpus.

HOUSEKEEPER: There, he's at it again!

STUDENT: How long has it been going on?

NIECE: Weeks.

HOUSEKEEPER: Months.

NIECE: Not the fighting.

HOUSEKEEPER: No, that's new. But these other capers.

STUDENT: What other capers?

HOUSEKEEPER: Books!

STUDENT: What does he do with them?

HOUSEKEEPER: Reads them, what do you think!

STUDENT: That's harmless enough.

HOUSEKEEPER: You think so! Well, you're a student, you're
at it yourself, may God help you. But they've done for my
master, poor Senor Quixada.

STUDENT: Books have?

HOUSEKEEPER: He can't leave them alone. He's read so much

he's addled his brain. The Knight of this and the Knight of that, giants and wizards and I don't know what else, till he thinks they're all in the room with him. Listen to him again! He's slashed his bedclothes to ribbons, I daren't go in there now, in case he takes me for a dragon. Well, you're a student; you know everything; what's to be done?

They both look at him.

STUDENT: . . . you want my opinion?

He clears his throat.

Let us first examine the a priori assumption contained within the question itself. Supposing as it does the necessity for action, we must begin by discussing the logistical and existential implications of the, of the, of the—

HOUSEKEEPER: Thank you very much. Here come his friends the Priest and the barber, maybe they'll be more help.

The PRIEST *and* NICHOLAS *the barber enter.*

HOUSEKEEPER: Master Nicholas – reverend, I'm at my wits' end.

NICHOLAS *pats her hand.*

PRIEST: Where is he?

HOUSEKEEPER: In bed. Reading.

More noises from inside.

PRIEST: Could we perhaps observe him unobserved?

HOUSEKEEPER: This way. Only keep quiet if you don't want a sword through your guts —

NICHOLAS *puts a hand to his guts; the* PRIEST *crosses himself.*
The two of them go into the house with the HOUSEKEEPER.

NIECE: Don't you want to go and look?

STUDENT: If I were in bed I could do without people queueing up to stare at me.

He opens a book and pretends to read.

NIECE: They only want to help him.

STUDENT: They might do that by leaving him be.

NIECE: Would you like *your* uncle to be a laughing stock?

STUDENT: If people aren't doing any harm they should be left alone. I believe in freedom.

NIECE: You're so impractical.

STUDENT: Maybe I am.

He returns to his book. The PRIEST, NICHOLAS *and the* HOUSEKEEPER *come out again, shaking their heads.*

PRIEST: So sad, so sad . . .

NICHOLAS: A crying shame . . .

HOUSEKEEPER: Did you see how he thrashed about?

PRIEST: I thank God I wasn't inside that pillow.

NICHOLAS: What pillow? Didn't you hear? That was the Giant of the Boiling Lake.

PRIEST: The only giant to spout feathers when you chop his head off.

NICHOLAS *and the* PRIEST *laugh. The* PRIEST *suddenly stops laughing.*

PRIEST: So sad.

NICHOLAS: A crying shame.

They look solemn.

NIECE: He used to be such a dignified man . . .

She cries. The PRIEST *consoles her.*

PRIEST: There, there.

NICHOLAS *decides to console the* HOUSEKEEPER.

NICHOLAS: There, there. Just you leave it to us.

HOUSEKEEPER: I wondered if you could exercise him.

PRIEST: Exercise him?

HOUSEKEEPER: Wave some incense around in there, throw holy water at him . . .

PRIEST: No, no, it's his brain. Inflammation of the brain due to a surfeit of literature, that's the trouble, wouldn't you say, Nicholas?

NICHOLAS: No, no, His blood's too hot, Too hot and too much of it. This is what I'd do: tie him to the bed; cold compresses on his forehead, and you can do a bit of preaching at him at the same time, since he can't get away; apply a dozen or two of leeches; when they've had their fill, take an ice-cold bath —

STUDENT: Or you could leave him alone.

NICHOLAS: Who's this?

HOUSEKEEPER: A student.

NICHOLAS: Get back to your lessons. As I was saying, after the leeches —

PRIEST: He's stopped.

NICHOLAS: Knocked himself out maybe, ho ho.

PRIEST: It's no laughing matter.

NICHOLAS: Oh, I agree.

NIECE: And now he's talking of going away.

PRIEST: Away where?

NIECE: As a Knight Errant.

NICHOLAS: At his age?

PRIEST: In this age?

NIECE: He says the world is full of evil.

PRIEST: What does he think the Church is for?

NIECE: There's no arguing with him.

HOUSEKEEPER: He's found a lot of old bits of rusty armour in the attic. His great grandfather's. He's been trying it on.

PRIEST: This sounds serious. Nicholas, we must give this our earnest consideration. What with your practicality and my divine inspiration we ought to be able to cook something up.

Two institutions exist to deal with evil – the Church, to condemn, and its physical arm, the Holy Brotherhood, to castigate. For an individual to take on the job smells to me of sacrilege. Come, let's put our minds to it over a bottle.

NICHOLAS: That's a good idea for a start.

He pats the HOUSEKEEPER's *hand.*

Don't you worry about a thing.

PRIEST (*patting the* NIECE's *hand*): Keep us informed; we'll think of something.

The PRIEST *and* NICHOLAS *leave.*

HOUSEKEEPER (*looking at the* STUDENT): He's right. If people did a bit less reading and left things to the authorities, there'd be less trouble in the world.

She goes inside.

STUDENT: As for your uncle being a laughing stock, I've been one all my life and no one seems bothered about it.

He looks hopefully at the NIECE. *She says nothing.*

DON QUIXOTE *comes out, dressed in shirt and breeches, carrying an old helmet for which he is fashioning a cardboard visor, which he is attaching with a ribbon. He sits on the bench outside the door and gives his attention to it.*

NIECE: What do you want with that old armour, Uncle?

DON QUIXOTE: To protect me from my enemies, my child.

NIECE: But you haven't any enemies.

DON QUIXOTE: Are there no evil beings left in the world then?

NIECE: Yes, but —

DON QUIXOTE: Would you have them be my friends?

NIECE: No, but —. Oh . . .

She goes. The STUDENT *looks at* DON QUIXOTE *from over his book.*

STUDENT: Senor...

DON QUIXOTE: Hold this a moment, I pray you.

STUDENT: Excuse me, Senor, but I'm against violence. I think the Scriptures are quite clear on that point, in tone if not in matter. Personally, I look at the question from a pragmatical point of view. I'm not sure the sword is the most efficient way to win battles.

DON QUIXOTE: How else?

STUDENT: Rational argument? Discussion?

DON QUIXOTE: Have you ever won an argument, my friend?

STUDENT: Well, no, but —

DON QUIXOTE: Or convinced your opponent in discussion?

STUDENT: No, but I'm exceptional.

DON QUIXOTE: I think not.

STUDENT: Well ... Of course, we must all do as we think best ...

He leaves, after the NIECE, *tripping over his feet.* DON QUIXOTE *continues with his work.* SANCHO PANZA *enters the yard. He makes sure no one else is about before he goes over to* DON QUIXOTE.

SANCHO: Senor Quixada. Your honour —

DON QUIXOTE: Not Quixada.

SANCHO: Yes, your honour, that's your name, Quixada ...

DON QUIXOTE: No longer. Quixada seemed to me not to have a Knightly ring to it. From now on you must call me 'Don Quixote of La Mancha'.

SANCHO: I'll try, Senor Quixada.

DON QUIXOTE: Quixote. And my horse you must call 'Rozinante.'

SANCHO: What horse?

DON QUIXOTE: The one in my stable.

SANCHO: That old — That one? Ah . . . Not Pedro?

DON QUIXOTE: Pedro hardly does justice to his unique qualities.

SANCHO: That's true. 'Unique' is good, if it means what I think it means, that I've never seen another horse like it nor hope to. Ronizante then.

DON QUIXOTE: Rozinante.

SANCHO: And if I have to call myself something, what'll that be?

DON QUIXOTE: Sancho Panza, of course. A squire is but a Squire, Sancho; and in all the Chivalries I've read there's hardly a mention of a Squire's name, so it's obviously of little importance.

SANCHO: Except to the Squire. Whereas a horse is a horse, I see that, that's logical. But touching on this 'Squire', your honour, as to *Squire* —

DON QUIXOTE: Have you decided?

SANCHO: It's difficult, your honour. I usually talk things over with my good wife; but since you made me swear I'd keep it a secret I'd no one to talk it over with but myself, and I find I'm not much help. One Sancho Panza's bad enough, but two together's like two cats in a bag, all spit and nothing decided.

DON QUIXOTE: Don't you want to serve me?

SANCHO: I do, your honour. Only it's a big step. Never having set foot outside the village, it's a big step, and I'm not sure I'm up to it.

DON QUIXOTE: Then I must go alone.

SANCHO: I don't like to think of you on your own out there . . .

DON QUIXOTE: Decide, then; one way or the other.

SANCHO: You made it sound pretty good when you talked about it last, I remember that . . . Look, your honour, if I wait for Sancho Panza to make up his mind we'll both wait till doomsday; so, being a Christian, I'll leave the choice to Him that made me; I'll toss for it. Heads I go, tails I stay. Is that fair?

DON QUIXOTE: As you wish.

SANCHO: Right. Head I stay, tails I go.

He fishes for a coin, without much hope. DON QUIXOTE *gives him one. He tosses it.*

DON QUIXOTE: Tails.

SANCHO: Ah . . . Tails . . . What was tails?

DON QUIXOTE: You come with me, Sancho.

SANCHO: I go with you . . . Well then, I go with you.

DON QUIXOTE: Good. We shall leave at once.

SANCHO: At once, right, Master . . . (*He double takes.*)

Which at once? This – present – at once?

That is to say, *now*?

DON QUIXOTE: Why not?

SANCHO: Why not, Why not? Think, think . . . !

DON QUIXOTE: Well?

SANCHO: Let's go, your honour.

They go.

SCENE TWO

The road. A hot afternoon. DON QUIXOTE *enters slowly on his horse Rozinante, followed some paces behind by* SANCHO *leading his ass.* SANCHO *is mopping his brow. His ass suddenly stops.*

SANCHO: Your honour!

    DON QUIXOTE *stops and looks round.*

My ass has stopped.

DON QUIXOTE: Then start it, Sancho, and don't disturb me when my thoughts are on matters of chivalry.

SANCHO: Easier said than done. This is no ordinary ass. This is an ass with common sense. She's been walking all day without food or drink, and every minute the road's got dustier and the sun's got hotter. And now she's stopped. What she's saying is, she won't budge another inch without some promise for the immediate future. Which goes to show she's got more common sense than some I could name, including me.

DON QUIXOTE: Are you her master or not?

SANCHO: Not. We're good friends, that's all.

DON QUIXOTE: Very well. We'll rest here. But I don't intend to be dictated to by an ass.

SANCHO: I'll tell her.

    DON QUIXOTE *dismounts.* SANCHO *sits down.*

DON QUIXOTE: I don't understand it. Sancho. In the books

of chivalry and the romances the roads are thick with giants, dragons, evil knights, maidens chained to trees, two-headed serpents — Where *are* they all?

SANCHO: Let's not be impatient.

DON QUIXOTE: Yes, you are right. I'm too eager to meet these frightful adversaries.

SANCHO: You are, master, you are. Don't worry; as soon as these serpents and dragons hear you're in the district they'll be on you as thick as fleas, I daresay.

DON QUIXOTE: Thank you, Sancho.

SANCHO: You're welcome.

DON QUIXOTE: But there is another thing which troubles me more.

SANCHO: What's that?

DON QUIXOTE: I've not been dubbed.

SANCHO: What's 'dubbed'?

DON QUIXOTE: A *Knight*, dubbed a Knight. Until I am, I'm only a shadow of one.

SANCHO: Well how does it work, this dubbing? I've done most jobs, from mending a roof to delivering a sow of piglets, so I don't mind having a try at it.

DON QUIXOTE: It's a simple ritual. A man of noble birth reads certain passages while I kneel before him; then he strikes me with his palm and the flat of his sword and pronounces me a Knight.

SANCHO: That's me out of it then. The striking I could manage, that's my line of country; the snags are the noble birth, which I couldn't swear to, not knowing exactly who my father was: and the reading, which is not one of my accompaniments, apart from being able to tell an 'A' from a 'B' one shot in every two.

Voices are heard offstage. Presently a shepherd LAD *enters, half-running.*

LAD: Don't beat me any more, master, I won't do it again!

DON QUIXOTE *stands up and reaches for his lance. The* FARMER'S *voice is heard.*

FARMER: Come back, you lazy good-for-nothing, and let me knock the living daylights out of you!

The FARMER *enters, his stick raised, and grabs the* LAD *by the scruff of the neck.*

DON QUIXOTE: Hold!

The FARMER *freezes in astonishment, his stick raised over the* LAD.

False Knight! Those who oppress the weak must account for it to me!

FARMER: And who the devil are you?

DON QUIXOTE: I am Don Quixote of La Mancha! (*He points his lance at the* FARMER.) Well may you cringe before my name. Explain your conduct, churl, before I run you through.

FARMER: If you'll put that thing a bit farther from my throat, I will. This bone-idle wretch is paid to look after my sheep. And what happens? Every day there's one more missing and every day he swears he knows nothing about it. So I've lost all patience with him and I'm taking it out on his hide. What's wrong with that?

DON QUIXOTE: What have you to say, lad?

LAD: Can I help it if his flock's too big to look after properly? the mean old devil? As for paying me, he hasn't done that in nine months.

FARMER: You want me to *pay* for losing my sheep? You do that well enough for nothing!

DON QUIXOTE: Silence! What does he owe you?

B

LAD: Nine months at seven reals a month. Lord knows what that comes to.

DON QUIXOTE: Sixty-three reals.

FARMER: Fifty-three.

DON QUIXOTE: Sixty-three!

FARMER: And what about the pair of shoes I bought you, and the cost of two blood-lettings when you were ill that time? I've been like a father to this lad, and this is the thanks I get.

DON QUIXOTE: This is my verdict. His wearing out of your shoe-leather with his feet will pay for your wearing out his back with your stick. And the two blood-lettings when he was ill will go against the blood you drew with your stick when he was well. And now give him the sixty-three reals or breathe your last.

FARMER: I haven't got it on me. I'll pay him when I get him home.

LAD: Ho ho!

DON QUIXOTE: On your word as a Knight.

FARMER: On my word as a Knight, I'll pay him back when I get him home. With interest too.

LAD: With his stick, that's how he'll pay me. You can't trust *him*, sir!

DON QUIXOTE: I have his word as a Knight.

LAD: But he's not a Knight!

DON QUIXOTE: Well, he's a landowner. Landowners too have their code of behaviour.

FARMER: It's good to meet a trusting man, sir Knight, they're few and far between, I can tell you.

LAD: I should think they are with you around!

The FARMER *makes as if to cuff him, then changes the gesture to a patting of his head.*

FARMER: Come on, then, my angel, come home and be paid—
(Quietly) – out. *(He leads the* LAD *away.)*

LAD *(sadly)*: Oh, sir, you've got a lot to learn . . .
The LAD *and* THE FARMER *go.*

DON QUIXOTE: Another good deed done, another wrong righted. If only all were as I am, the world would be a better place.

SANCHO: Your honour . . .

DON QUIXOTE: What is it?

SANCHO: It could be my empty belly tormenting me with visions, but do you see what I see?

DON QUIXOTE: Where?

SANCHO: There.

DON QUIXOTE: A castle!

SANCHO: Then it's not one vision, but two. What I see is more like a pigsty than a castle, but it could just be an inn.

DON QUIXOTE: Don't you see the battlements, and the turrets, with pennants flying?

SANCHO: Pennants? Master there's something funny here; what I see is a row of washing out to dry.

DON QUIXOTE: Don't contradict me, Sancho, you know nothing of these things. Help me mount, quickly.
SANCHO helps him on to Rozinante.
Take heed, all you within, for there is about to enter your gates that most valiant and awe-inspiring Knight, Don Quixote of La Mancha —
He rides off.

SANCHO *(to his ass)*: It's a pigsty. But it's better than nothing.
He follows with his ass.

SCENE THREE

The stableyard of the Inn, with the Inn behind it. A table and benches against the wall, and a horse-trough. The sun is setting.

DON QUIXOTE enters, and stops outside the courtyard. SANCHO comes on behind him.

SANCHO: What are we waiting for?

DON QUIXOTE: A Knight never enters a castle unannounced; surely you know that.

SANCHO: Oh well, yes . . .

Pause.

Only what if they don't see us?

DON QUIXOTE: Of course they'll see us. There's a dwarf on the battlements.

SANCHO scratches his head.

In all the chivalries a dwarf on the battlements blows his trumpet at the approach of strangers. The fellow must have fallen asleep.

SANCHO: Or fallen off the battlements when he found there weren't any . . .

A horn is blown.

DON QUIXOTE: There! We are announced.

SANCHO: Your honour. That's a swineherd calling the pigs in. Look, there he is.

DON QUIXOTE: You've been too long in the sun, Sancho.

SANCHO: Well, have it your way. It can be the Angel Gabriel if it gets us inside for something to eat.

DON QUIXOTE: Listen, they are lowering the drawbridge.

SANCHO: My stomach calling out for food.

DON QUIXOTE: What?

SANCHO: It's a drawbridge, it's a drawbridge.

Quiet now, guts, or he'll think they've taken it up again.

They approach the inn. A trollop, MARIA by name, comes round the corner of the inn into the stableyard. She stops and screams. DON QUIXOTE rides towards her.

DON QUIXOTE: Beauteous damsel —

MARIA: Get away! Don't you touch me!

DON QUIXOTE: Fear not my awesome aspect, lady. For by the order of chivalry which I profess I exist but to serve maidens such as you.

MARIA stares openmouthed for a moment, then rolls up with laughter.

I see nothing to laugh at.

MARIA: You're not standing where I am.

DON QUIXOTE: Fair ingrate, beauty without civility —

She whoops with laughter again. The INNKEEPER comes out of the inn followed by his WIFE. He begins to laugh. DON QUIXOTE lowers his lance.

Laugh at me, fellow, and you'll not live to regret it!

SANCHO, who has been grinning in sympathy, stops. The INNKEEPER turns at once to his wife.

INNKEEPER: Stop insulting the gentleman! What are you thinking of?

He flails at MARIA with his dishcloth. His WIFE follows suit.

WIFE: You trollop.

INNKEEPER: If it's bed and board you're after, Sir Knight,

you've come to the right place, if you don't mind roughing it a bit.

WIFE: It's pot-luck here and no faldelals!

DON QUIXOTE: I thank you for your courtesy, Sir Castellan, and your fair duchess. I shall accept with gratitude what you are pleased to offer.

INNKEEPER: What's he say? (*To his* WIFE.)

WIFE: What's he say? (*To Sancho.*)

SANCHO: He says just bring the grub and we'll say no more about it.

INNKEEPER: Maria! Help the gallant Knight off his —
    He looks at Rozinante.

WIFE: — *horse.* Look sharp or I'll lay about you.

INNKEEPER: And then bring some food
    MARIA *helps* DON QUIXOTE *off Rozinante, trying not to giggle.*

WIFE: You slut.

INNKEEPER: We can find you a bit of boiled salt cod and some bread, take it . . .

WIFE: Or leave it.

SANCHO: We'll take it.

    The INNKEEPER *takes Rozinante by the halter and leads him and the ass off to the stables. His wife sets the table, listening meanwhile.*

DON QUIXOTE: Take care of my steed, for he is the finest in the world! Would it please you, beauteous damsel, to assist in divesting me of my armour, for I am sore weary.

    MARIA *looks blank.*

SANCHO: Take his armour off.

WIFE: Do what the gentleman asks. Are you deaf?

    MARIA *begins to do so.*

DON QUIXOTE: What is your name, fair lady?

MARIA: Who, me? Maria.

DON QUIXOTE: From now on you must call yourself – Dona Maritornes, a title more in keeping with your grace and beauty.

MARIA: What?

SANCHO: Dona Maritornes.

WIFE: Do as you're told, you baggage.

DON QUIXOTE: I am that Knight Don Quixote of La Mancha of whose exploits you have heard tell.

SANCHO: Yes.

(*Maria looks round at the Innkeeper's wife, bemused.*)

WIFE: Say yes if the gentleman wants you to!

MARIA: Oh. Yes.

DON QUIXOTE: Fain would I emblazon your name on my shield as in my heart, since I see that you look upon me with eyes – may I say it? – not entirely devoid of love; but alas, it cannot be. My heart is tied to another, that cruel tyrant of my affections, the Lady Dulcinea del Toboso.

MARIA (*appealing to the wife*): Oh, yes . . . I can't get this *off*. Not without taking his head off.

The WIFE *comes to look.*

WIFE: DOLT! Cut the ribbons.

DON QUIXOTE: What!

WIFE (*bringing out scissors*): We'll have to cut your ribbons, dear.

MARIA: You won't get that thing off without.

DON QUIXOTE: I will not have my ribbons cut.

SANCHO: Now, your honour, be reasonable.

DON QUIXOTE: I will not have my ribbons cut.

SANCHO: But she can't get your helmet off!

DON QUIXOTE: Then it must stay on.

SANCHO (*to* MARIA): Leave it, leave it.

WIFE: Leave it.

MARIA: How's he gonna eat, then?

WIFE: How's he gonna eat!

SANCHO: That's his problem.

WIFE: Mind your own business.

> *The* INNKEEPER *has brought out food, which she sets on the table and then goes into the inn again.*

SANCHO: God be praised, FOOD!

Come, your honour, let's tuck in while the going's good. By the smell of that fish it's been too long in the world already.

DON QUIXOTE: I'll eat it whatever it be. Sancho, for it comes most opportunely.

SANCHO: True. And as they say everything's for the best, let's thank God for our empty bellies; because without mine I'd be tempted to think this the most disgusting dish of stinking catfood I ever fell upon.

> *He tucks in and drinks.* DON QUIXOTE *tries to eat, but each time his visor snaps shut and he cannot get the food over the top of it.* MARIA *feeds him.*

SANCHO: Try the wine, it's nearly drinkable.

> DON QUIXOTE *tries to drink; it's impossible.*

WIFE: Help the gentleman.

MARIA: Here, let me.

> *She pours wine into his helmet,* DON QUIXOTE *chokes.*

WIFE: Don't drown him, baggage, we haven't been paid yet! Get a funnel.

> *She fetches a funnel, and they pour wine into* DON QUIXOTE. SANCHO *belches. The* INNKEEPER *returns.*

SANCHO: My master and me give you thanks.

INNKEEPER: What for?

SANCHO: For presenting us with the family heirloom.

INNKEEPER: Heirloom?

SANCHO: This fish.

INNKEEPER: You don't have to eat it.

SANCHO: Wrong, I do.

INNKEEPER: About your business, you two!

   The INNKEEPER *sits next to* SANCHO.

INNKEEPER: Your master . . . He's a bit mad, is he? . . .

SANCHO: What! He's no more mad than this fish stinks.

INNKEEPER: That's prime fish!

SANCHO: Well, there's your answer. The fact is, he's an educated man. What's mad to ignorant pigs like you – and me – don't have to be mad to an educated gentleman.

INNKEEPER: Mad is mad

SANCHO: No, you're wrong there. If a man talks gibberish you say he's mad; but if it turns out to be Latin, where are you then and who's the idiot?

INNKEEPER: So he's not mad.

SANCHO: Oh, he's mad. But *educated* mad. So I'll thank you to humour him and keep him sweet for me; mad or not, I've got to live with it.

INNKEEPER: Has he got money?

SANCHO: Did you ever hear of a *Don* without money?

INNKEEPER: I'll humour him.

DON QUIXOTE: Sir Castellan!

INNKEEPER: At your service, Sir Knight

   He winks at SANCHO. DON QUIXOTE *gets up and goes to him, falling on his knees.*

DON QUIXOTE: Never will I rise from this spot until you promise to grant me the boon which I crave!

SANCHO: Promise.

INNKEEPER: I promise. What is it?

DON QUIXOTE: That in the morning you dub me Knight.

> *The* INNKEEPER *looks at* SANCHO, *who nods.*

INNKEEPER: I'll do that. Mind you, Wednesday's my usual day for dubbing Knights, but I'll stretch a point.

DON QUIXOTE: Now, if you will show my Squire his quarters, I shall begin my vigil in the chapel.

INNKEEPER: What chapel?

DON QUIXOTE: You must know, Sir Castellan, that the night before being knighted the Knight spends the night watching over his armour in the castle chapel.

SANCHO: That's four nights gone already.

INNKEEPER: Ah, now you've caught me on the hop there. The chapel's under repair just now.

DON QUIXOTE: That matters not. Lead me there.

INNKEEPER: That's to say, it's being reconsecrated. It was desecrated by vandals.

DON QUIXOTE: Then have your Priest see to it at once. I pray.

INNKEEPER: Ah, the Priest's away, you see, er . . .

SANCHO: Delivering a cow of calf.

INNKEEPER: Delivering a cow of calf.

DON QUIXOTE: The Priest?

INNKEEPER: He's a Jack-of-all-trades. Best midwife in the district. He does the christening at the same time, you see, all for the one price, so he's much sought after.

> SANCHO *is killing himself.*

DON QUIXOTE: Calves are christened in this district?

INNKEEPER: Calves, piglets, chicks . . . We're a very sanctimonious lot round here, Sir Knight.

SANCHO: The world's full of wonders, your honour.

DON QUIXOTE: It is indeed.

INNKEEPER: As for your vigil, you don't need a chapel for a vigil. I never vidgeled in a chapel.

DON QUIXOTE: Did you not?

INNKEEPER: Never in my life. I vidgeled here in the castle courtyard; by the . . . horsetrough. Since then I've rescued more maidens than you've had hot dinners, so it can't have done me any harm. Best vidgeling trough in the district that one.

DON QUIXOTE: Very well. Leave me now, Sancho. Go to bed.

DON QUIXOTE *begins to place his armour on the trough.*

SANCHO: You're not staying out here all night, your honour?

DON QUIXOTE: Yes.

SANCHO: In the cold? You'll catch your death. I'll fetch a blanket.

DON QUIXOTE: Knights do not do vigils in blankets.

SANCHO: I don't like to leave you . . .

DON QUIXOTE: Go to bed, Sancho.

SANCHO *shrugs.*

INNKEEPER: There's a mattress in the loft. We're a bit full tonight. Take it.

WIFE (*window*): Or leave it.

SANCHO: I'll take it. I just hope your mattress is softer than your fish was fresh.

INNKEEPER: That was prime fish!

SANCHO: And there's *my* answer. But I'm tired enough for it to feel like the lap of an angel if it's a bag full of rocks I'm on. Lead on, Innkeeper.

INNKEEPER: Sir Castellan to you.

SANCHO: Goodnight, your honour. I'll keep a place in case you change your mind.

He follows the INNKEEPER *into the inn.* DON QUIXOTE *doesn't notice their going. He buckles on his shield and, carrying his lance, he walks to and fro in front of the trough. It is now dark, with a moon.* A CARRIER *comes into the yard from outside.*

CARRIER: Hallo! Anyone about!

This to the Inn. DON QUIXOTE *ignores him. The* CARRIER *sees the wine on the table and drinks some.*

MARIA *comes out again.*

MARIA: Oh, it's you back again.

CARRIER: That's a nice way to greet me after six months away. Give us a kiss.

MARIA: Leave me be. You turn up once in a blue moon and expect me to jump into your arms. And in the morning you'll push off again without saying goodbye. And what about that present you promised me last time?

The CARRIER *takes out a string of beads and dangles them in front of her. She makes a grab, but he jerks them out of reach.*

CARRIER: Real stones, they are.

MARIA: I bet. Let's have a look.

The CARRIER *keeps them out of her reach.*

CARRIER: Where do I sleep?

MARIA: In the loft. We're full up tonight.

The CARRIER *snatches a kiss.*

CARRIER: You can come and pay me a visit.

MARIA: I'll think about it.

She makes another grab for the beads.

CARRIER: I'll keep these till then.

MARIA: Pig.

CARRIER: And I want something to eat.

MARIA: Inside.

CARRIER: Get it ready. I'll just water my mules.

MARIA goes in. The CARRIER goes off, and returns with a bucket. He goes to the trough. He sees the armour on it and goes to remove it.

DON QUIXOTE: Touch not that armour!

CARRIER: Eh?

DON QUIXOTE: Take heed what you do, rash Knight, or prepare to forfeit your life!

The CARRIER stares at him for a moment, then turns back to the trough, lifts off some of the armour and throws it aside with a crash. DON QUIXOTE raises his eyes to heaven.

DON QUIXOTE: Succour your Knight, my lady Dulcinea, and fail me not in this my first affray!

So saying, he raises his lance in both hands and brings it down on the CARRIER's head. The CARRIER howls and falls to the ground. DON QUIXOTE picks up the armour to put it back. The CARRIER gets up and boots DON QUIXOTE in the seat.

I am attacked!

He swings round. The CARRIER is knocked over again as the lance sweeps round and hits the side off his head. He gets up immediately and, taking the breastplate, slams it down on DON QUIXOTE's head. DON QUIXOTE's helmet comes off, and he falls senseless. The CARRIER begins to belabour him.

CARRIER: Keep all the water to yourself, would you!

MARIA comes running out.

MARIA: Leave the poor old man alone! He's not right in the head!

CARRIER: Never mind *his* head, what about *my* head!

MARIA: Leave him be, you brute!

She belabours the CARRIER.

CARRIER: All *right!*

The CARRIER *takes his bucket full of water and goes.* MARIA *stoops over* DON QUIXOTE. *He comes to.*

DON QUIXOTE: What is this vision? Is it an angel?

MARIA: It's me, sir. Are you all right.

DON QUIXOTE: Had it not been for the other two —

MARIA: What other two?

DON QUIXOTE: Three or four set on me from behind. Did you not see them?

MARIA: Oh. Yes. Five or six I should think. Poor old man . . .

SANCHO *comes out with the* INNKEEPER.

SANCHO: Master, are you hurt?

INNKEEPER: What's going on? You causing trouble again, Maria, cos if you are —

DON QUIXOTE: I was set upon by a band of criminals.

SANCHO *and the* INNKEEPER *look at* MARIA. *She holds up one finger.*

Let me tell you, Sir Castellan, that if I am attacked again within your castle I shall spare the life of no one.

He raises his voice.

Be warned, all ye who lurk in the shadows! Be warned!

INNKEEPER: Keep your voice down. I don't want any trouble. I've got an officer of the Holy Brotherhood staying the night, he'd just love to put me out of business. Look, you've done your vigil; go to bed now and let's get some sleep.

DON QUIXOTE: What of my armour?

INNKEEPER: I'll guard your – armour.

Together MARIA *and* SANCHO *get him to his feet.*

DON QUIXOTE: With your life.

INNKEEPER: With my life.

SANCHO: Take my advice, master; leave the mattress and sleep on the boards; they're softer.

The three go into the inn. The INNKEEPER *waits a moment, knocks the rest of the armour off the trough and goes indoors.*

SCENE FOUR

The loft of the Inn.

In the shaft of moonlight which comes through a window can be seen three figures asleep on the floor: the CARRIER, SANCHO *next to him and, nearest the trap-door,* DON QUIXOTE. *All three are snoring. The trap-door opens and* MARIA *appears.*

MARIA (*whispers*): Where are you?

    The pig's asleep. With my present under the pillow, I bet.

    She begins to tiptoe across the loft, hands outstretched.

Where *are* you?

    DON QUIXOTE *sits up.*

DON QUIXOTE: Look no further, beauteous lady.

    He stretches out his arms and catches her hand. She trips over his mattress and falls on top of him with a little scream.

MARIA: Let me go . . .

DON QUIXOTE: Unhappy lady, I feared you might come to me to confess your love. But alas, it cannot be, since I am bound by the plighted faith I have given to the peerless Dulcinea del Tobosa.

MARIA: I don't know what you're talking about. Let *go* of me!

    The CARRIER *wakes up.*

CARRIER: What's going on? Maria?

MARIA: Yes. No.

DON QUIXOTE: Who's there? Who dares to enter my bed-chamber unannounced?

CARRIER: What? You again! First my water and now my girl. I'll do for you once and for all.

He steps on SANCHO, *who yells out in his sleep, and then brings his fists down on* DON QUIXOTE'*s head.* DON QUIXOTE *collapses senseless.*

MARIA: Oh, you brute! How can you hit a defenceless man!

CARRIER: I'll show you how!

He tramples up and down on DON QUIXOTE.

CARRIER: That's for the water. And that's for Maria. And that's for waking me up. And that's for —

The INNKEEPER'*s voice is heard, and that of his wife.*

INNKEEPER: What's going on up there!

WIFE: Maria, you up to your tricks?

MARIA: If they find me here they'll kill me

She dives into the nearest hiding place, which is under SANCHO'*s blanket, where she curls up in a quaking ball, as the* INNKEEPER'*s head appears, followed by his wife.* SANCHO *half-wakes up with a yell, and sits up.*

SANCHO: Gerroff! Warrisit! Help! There's a creature in my bed! Demons master! Dragons!

Yelling, he begins to lay about him wildly, some of the blows connecting with MARIA.

MARIA: Ow! Lay off!

She appears from under the blanket and begins to lay into SANCHO, *who therefore hits back even more wildly.*

CARRIER: The devil! Here's another one at it! No one bashes my girl but me!

He jumps off DON QUIXOTE *on to* SANCHO'*s mattress and begins to belabour* SANCHO.

C

WIFE: It *is* you again, you trollop!

INNKEEPER: I'll give you what for!

They jump in and begin to beat MARIA. *The* CARRIER *beats the* INNKEEPER, SANCHO *beats the* CARRIER, *etc.*

A gaunt figure appears at the trap-door, in a night-shirt and night-cap, holding up a lantern. He has a staff in his other hand. He is an OFFICER *of the Holy Brotherhood.*

OFFICER: Hold in the name of justice! Hold in the name of the Holy Brotherhood.

He comes into the loft.

INNKEEPER: It's the Officer!

The INNKEEPER, *his* WIFE *and* MARIA *scuttle with incredible speed across the loft and through the trap-door, while the* CARRIER *returns to his mattress and under the blanket in one leap, where he immediately starts to snore.* SANCHO *sits feeling his bruises and groaning. The* OFFICER *lifts* DON QUIXOTE'S *head by the beard and examines it by the light of the lantern. He lets it fall again.*

OFFICER: Here is a dead man! Shut the inn gate! Murder! Let no one leave!

SANCHO: Dead?

He stops groaning and kneels by DON QUIXOTE'S *side.*

Master? Your honour?

OFFICER: Never fear! I shall apprehend the murderer.

SANCHO: Will that bring him back to life then?

Your honour? Brave Knight, sir? Noble Knight, sir . . .?

He bows his head till it touches the mattress. DON QUIXOTE *sits up with a groan.*

DON QUIXOTE: Where am I?

SANCHO: Are you alive then?

OFFICER (*disappointed*): Oh, you're alive.

DON QUIXOTE: I have been enchanted, Sancho.

OFFICER: The poor fellow's out of his wits.

DON QUIXOTE: I've more wits than you, lout, and in a moment I'll teach you to show respect for the valiant Don Quixote!

SANCHO: Ssh! Master, it's the Holy Brotherhood!

OFFICER: So much for gratitude. Well, this is for wasting my time pretending to be dead.

He brings his staff down on DON QUIXOTE's *head, and leaves.* DON QUIXOTE *again falls senseless.*

SANCHO: Why can't you keep your mouth shut, your honour?

SCENE FIVE

The Inn yard. Morning. A cock is crowing.

The CARRIER *comes out of the inn and crosses the yard, rubbing his bruises. He is followed by* MARIA, *rubbing her bruises.*

MARIA: But you promised.

CARRIER: Why should I give you presents? All I've got out of it's a mass of bruises.

MARIA: What about me? Whenever you turn up there's nothing but trouble.

They disappear, arguing.

The INNKEEPER *comes out of the inn, rubbing his bruises, followed by* DON QUIXOTE, *holding his head, and* SANCHO, *hobbling and rubbing his bruises.*

INNKEEPER: It took me half an hour to get that Officer to forget the matter. *Plus* putting something in his palm.

DON QUIXOTE: There's strong enchantment in this castle, Sir Castellan.

INNKEEPER: There wasn't till you turned up. So I'll thank you to get off the premises and take your enchantment with you.

DON QUIXOTE: Ah, Sancho, if we but had some of the magic balsam of which they speak in the chivalries, our aches and pains would disappear on the instant.

SANCHO: If that's the case, I could do with some of that just now.

INNKEEPER: Magic balsam, is it? I'll give you some magic ruddy balsam.

DON QUIXOTE: You have the secret, Sir Castellan?

The INNKEEPER *glares at them, then goes indoors.* SANCHO *groans.*

There were strange things last night, Sancho.

SANCHO: That's one way of putting it.

DON QUIXOTE: This you must not repeat to a soul, for the sake of the lady's honour; but last night the noble and haughty Dona Maritornes, the world's most beautiful damsel after my lady Dulcinea, came to my bedside weeping for love. I refused her, of course, with all delicacy, whereupon I was set upon by all the fiends in hell.

SANCHO: Not all, your honour; there were some left over for me.

DON QUIXOTE: That's impossible, Sancho. It's against the rules of chivalry to beat a Knight's Squire.

SANCHO: I wish they'd *play* it by the rules, then. But where Priests attend cows in labour what can you expect? Look sir, let's go before these fiends think up something else.

The INNKEEPER *comes out, with a basin full of liquid. His* WIFE *follows him out carrying her accounts-book, which she makes up.*

INNKEEPER: Here's your balsam

SANCHO *takes the basin, looks at it, smells it and is disgusted.*

SANCHO: After you.

He hands it to DON QUIXOTE, *who smells it.*

DON QUIXOTE: Is this the veritable balsam of Fierabras?

INNKEEPER: Try it and see.

DON QUIXOTE *drinks half the basinful, looked on with*

some surprise by SANCHO. *The* WIFE *notes it down. The* INN-
KEEPER *is enigmatic.* DON QUIXOTE *stands still for a moment,
waiting for it to take effect. The others also wait. Suddenly* DON
QUIXOTE *cries out, puts a hand to his stomach and another to his
seat, goes into a series of paroxysms and shoots offstage.*

DON QUIXOTE: Lady Dulcinea, protect me . . .!

SANCHO *looks on horrified, He turns to the* INNKEEPER,
who grins.

INNKEEPER: I'll get your animals and you can take yourselves
off. (*To the wife.*) Get that bill ready.

The INNKEEPER *goes.* SANCHO *looks at the basin. A cry
from* DON QUIXOTE *offstage.*

SANCHO: Devil take the stuff, I'll keep my bruises, Fierybrass
or no Fierybrass.

WIFE: How many helpings did you have of the fish?

Pause. No sound from DON QUIXOTE.

SANCHO: One too many.

WIFE: How many?

SANCHO: I've told you. ONE

Sir? Are you alive? Or dead again? If you've poisoned my
poor master —

DON QUIXOTE *appears.*

DON QUIXOTE: Cured, Sancho!

SANCHO: Cured?

DON QUIXOTE: My aches have gone. See.

He dances a little jig.

Drink, then. I've left you some.

SANCHO: So I see. Thanks very much.

He looks doubtfully at the basin.

DON QUIXOTE: Drink, Sancho.

SANCHO: I'm working up to it.

He picks up the basin, puts it down to hold his nose, tries to pick it up with one hand while holding his nose with the other; unsuccessful. He changes hands. Still no good.

Hard luck. With one more hand I could 've done it.

DON QUIXOTE *picks it up and holds it for him.* SANCHO, *after a couple of false tries, begins to drink. The* WIFE *notes it down. He flaps his free hand for* DON QUIXOTE *to take the basin away, but* DON QUIXOTE *holds it there and* SANCHO *has to drink the lot.* DON QUIXOTE *puts the basin down.* SANCHO *stands quite still, full of apprehension. A long pause.* SANCHO *cocks his head from side to side. He begins a slow smile. The smile turns to a look of consternation, grief, terror. He yells out, doubling up, puts both hands to his stomach and jerks erect, goes through a series of contortions and finishes up groaning on the ground.*

DON QUIXOTE: What ails you, Sancho?

The INNKEEPER *enters, leading Rozinante and the ass.*

INNKEEPER: My magic balsam's working I see, ho ho.

SANCHO: Curse you, Innkeeper. And curse your inn. And curse your stinking fish and your mattresses and your magic b-ow-!

He howls and doubles up again.

INNKEEPER: Here's your livestock, now you can take yourselves off and a good riddance.

DON QUIXOTE: You forget something, Sir Castellan.

INNKEEPER: What?

DON QUIXOTE: My dubbing.

INNKEEPER: The devil take your dubbing! It's a drubbing you'll get if you don't make yourselves scarce.

DON QUIXOTE: How?

He draws his sword.

INNKEEPER: All right, all right, have it your own way. So long as it's quick. Give us the sword.

DON QUIXOTE gives him the sword.

Kneel down.

He does so.

I hereby dub you —

DON QUIXOTE: The *book*, Sir Castellan.

INNKEEPER: Book? As you like, the book!

He takes the book from his wife. SANCHO sits up, groaning.

DON QUIXOTE: Feeling better, Sancho?

SANCHO: Ten times worse, if you must know.

DON QUIXOTE: I fear your constitution is of too base a metal. For you the balsam works in reverse.

SANCHO: You might have told me that before I took it.

The INNKEEPER returns with the book. He stands in front of DON QUIXOTE with the sword in one hand and the book in the other, and reads from it as if it were a litany.

INNKEEPER: 'On the fifth of March two bushels of corn and four of barley, on the seventeenth of March ditto . . .

He transfers the sword to the book hand so as to give DON QUIXOTE a slap at the side of the head.

'On the twentythird of March a bushel each of barley and corn and two sacks of hay, on the twentyninth three sacks of ditto . . .

He transfers the book and sword to the other hand so as to slap the other side of DON QUIXOTE's head.

INNKEEPER: 'Thirtieth of March three bushels of barley, on the first of April a bushel and a half of corn and two sacks each of hay and of stra-a-aaw.'

He then takes the sword and gives DON QUIXOTE a resounding thwack on each shoulder.

Arise, sir Knight.

DON QUIXOTE *rubs his shoulder with one hand. The* INNKEEPER *gives another thwack on the back of the hand.*
And that's for luck.

DON QUIXOTE *gets up. The* INNKEEPER *gives him back his sword.*
And now you can do something for *me*, Sir Knight.

DON QUIXOTE: What is that, Sir Castellan?

INNKEEPER: You can pay your bill and go.

He opens the book and reads from it, prompted by his WIFE.
Item, stabling and fodder for one ass and one so-called horse. Item, two dishes of prime boiled cod; item, shelter for one night with use of feather mattresses; item – What's this?

WIFE: Vidgeling trough.

INNKEEPER: Hire of one vidgeling trough.

DON QUIXOTE: What! You'd charge a Knight for staying at your castle!

INNKEEPER: I charge an addle-pated ass for putting up at my inn.

DON QUIXOTE: Inn?

WIFE: Inn.

INNKEEPER: Inn. Item, the conferring of one Knighthood; item, of magic balsam —

WIFE: For two.

DON QUIXOTE: Then I have been deceived.

INNKEEPER: That's your business. Just pay me what you owe me.

DON QUIXOTE: That I cannot do, for it is against the laws of Knight-errantry for a Knight to pay for his lodging. At least, I've never read of it in the chivalries.

INNKEEPER: To hell with your chivalries. Give me my money or it'll be the worse for you.

DON QUIXOTE *moves towards him. The* INNKEEPER *jumps out of the way. But* DON QUIXOTE *mounts Rozinante.*

DON QUIXOTE: If money is your only interest I have nothing more to say to you. Innkeeper, you are an ignorant lout.

So saying, he brandishes his lance and rides off.

Come, Sancho, there is work for us to do!

WIFE: Well? Do something.

SANCHO *staggers to his ass, holding his belly.*

INNKEEPER: And where d'you think you're going?

SANCHO (*with an attempt at dignity*): I go to attend my master.

He has a sudden attack of the gripes.

WIFE: Not till he pays he don't.

INNKEEPER: Not till you pay me, you don't.

SANCHO: After giving me that muck to drink! You heard what my Knight said, it's against the rules of chivalry. And as it goes for the Knight so it goes for the Squire. Item. And item, I haven't got a farthing on me and item, if I did have I'd give it to the devil before I gave it to you. Now kindly let me pass before I call Don Quixote of La Mancha to lay you out.

He starts to mount his ass, feeling he has acquitted himself well. The INNKEEPER'S WIFE, *however, grabs his foot before he can swing it over the ass's back, so that* SANCHO *lies athwart the ass.*

WIFE: Run out on a defenceless woman, would you? Help! Robbery! Help!

The CARRIER *appears with two or three others.*

CARRIER: What's he up to now?

INNKEEPER: Here's someone wants to leave without paying.

CARRIER: Sport, brothers! Fetch a blanket.

Some of them drag SANCHO *from his ass while one goes for a blanket. Two or three more come out from the inn.*

SANCHO: Unhand me, base knaves! Ow! Don Quixote! Master! Your honour! Here's someone to rescue!

Yelling, he is tossed up and down in the blanket while the others cheer.

WIFE: Don't tear the blanket.

He is finally let down. He staggers to his ass and mounts it with difficulty.

INNKEEPER: Now take yourself off.

WIFE: And another time, don't cause trouble in a quiet decent establishment.

SANCHO *rides off, groaning.*

SCENE SIX

The road.

DON QUIXOTE *is on Rozinante, who is stationary.* SANCHO
rides up on his ass, looking much the worse for wear. SANCHO
stops and more or less falls off the ass. He looks up at DON
QUIXOTE, *but* DON QUIXOTE *is staring intently at the ground.*

SANCHO: Your honour, I've got one or two bones to pick
with you.

DON QUIXOTE: I've been musing on this anthill, Sancho.
See how happily they scurry about, the innocent creatures,
each to his own task. Yet they know neither virtue nor vice,
neither chivalry nor baseness. They are as far from under-
standing chivalry as we are from knowing God.

    SANCHO *jumps up and down on the anthill, which does his
back no good.*

What are you doing?

SANCHO: Why should they have all the luck!

DON QUIXOTE: Well, let us get on. Today we shall rescue
some maiden from peril, I feel it in my bones.

SANCHO: Then I'm glad you've got bones left to feel it in
because it's more than I've got.

DON QUIXOTE: Come then, my good Squire.

    He begins to move off.

SANCHO: Not so fast if you don't mind, *Sir Knight*!

DON QUIXOTE *stops, surprised and angry at his tone.*

DON QUIXOTE: What!

SANCHO: That is to say – could we discuss one or two matters first?

DON QUIXOTE: We can talk while riding.

SANCHO: No, your honour.

DON QUIXOTE: Why not?

SANCHO: Well sir, there's discussing, which is still, and there's moving, which is not still but – moving. Which is to say, your theory in the one hand (*holding out a handful of theory*) and your *practice* in the other (*doing likewise with the other*); two of God's contraries which it's not for the likes of me to mix together. Ergo, speaking as a Christian —

DON QUIXOTE: Leave your ergo's to the Jesuits and let's get on.

SANCHO: Well then, not to put too fine a point on it, I'm a simple man and my brain-pan's not so big that it can incommodiate *one* thing at a time, let alone two. Ergo, I mean *so*, not to put too fine a point on it —

DON QUIXOTE: As you said.

SANCHO: — as I said, not to mince matters, if you insist on me moving and discussing at the same time I'll endeavour to serve you, as they say. Only don't blame me if I trip over my tongue and fall off one ass (*slapping his ass's rump*) on to the other. (*Slapping his own.*) That is to say, not to bandy words —

DON QUIXOTE: For heaven's sake, discuss what you like and be done with it.

SANCHO: Right. Item – as that knave of an innkeeper says, *item*: while you was studying ants and wondering who to rescue there was a prime bit of rescuing needed under your honour's nose; item, *me*. And if chilvary means a Knight lets his Squire get tossed in a blanket without raising a finger, then chilvary can go to blazes. Item —

DON QUIXOTE: I wanted to rescue you, Sancho, but a Knight cannot do battle with innkeepers.

SANCHO: Hard luck on me then. Next time I'll be more careful who I get done up by.

DON QUIXOTE: Is that all?

SANCHO: No, that was just the soup. Here's the meat. Your honour – I'm not saying I'm sorry I was ever fool enough to leave my wife and my village and set out with you for God knows where; only my memory's not the best in the world and I've forgot for the minute how you ever talked me into it. If you could just go over what you said then it might put some of the spirit back in me; and if I say it over to myself next time I'm having the life knocked out of me without anyone lifting a finger to help, it might take some of the sting out of it.

DON QUIXOTE: Gladly, Sancho; though I'm not sure now what I did say.

SANCHO: Then I'm done for.

DON QUIXOTE: I must have expounded on the virtues of a life dedicated to good; on the honour of serving a true and valorous Knight; and on the treasures stored up for us in Heaven.

SANCHO: Stop there. Treasure rings a bell. In heaven, was it? Wasn't there something a bit nearer home?

DON QUIXOTE: Nothing I can call to mind.

SANCHO: Oh . . .

He sighs.

DON QUIXOTE: I did, of course, promise you that when I win a kingdom through some great deed of valour I shall make you Governor of some Isle . . .

SANCHO: The Isle! That's the one! That's still on, is it?

DON QUIXOTE: I promise you, Sancho, you shall have your Isle, should we live.

SANCHO: Should we live . . . Did you say that 'should we live' bit last time?

DON QUIXOTE: If we perish in a just cause, surely that is worth more than all the Isles.

SANCHO: Oh, well, yes . . . I tell you what, master, I've got a small memory so I'll just hang on to the Isle bit and the rest can go hang itself. And next time I'm in the middle of a beating and your honour can't help me out of it, if you'd just yell out 'Isle' it'll do nearly as well if not better. And now I've done discussing and I'm ready to move. I don't want someone else grabbing my Isle before we get there.

They begin to move off. DON QUIXOTE *stops.*

DON QUIXOTE: Fortune is guiding our affairs, friend Sancho. Look yonder!

SANCHO *looks.*

SANCHO: What am I supposed to be looking at?

DON QUIXOTE: Do you not see? Giants! Thirty or more. You see how little cause you had for despondency. For when I have done battle with them and taken all their lives, their riches will be ours; for it's quite correct for a Knight to take the treasure of those he vanquishes, as in the chivalries.

SANCHO: That's fine, master, I'm in agreement with that. The only thing is – what giants?

DON QUIXOTE: *There, there,* are you blind? With the long arms.

SANCHO: Your honour – those are windmills.

DON QUIXOTE: Sancho, if you are afraid, go back home. As for me, my course is clear.

SANCHO: Look, the wind's coming up, don't you see their sails going round?

DON QUIXOTE: Fly not, vile cowards, for I am but a single cavalier! But though you have more arms than the giant Briareus, I shall lay you low! I commend me to my lady Dulcinea . . . !

He gallops off. SANCHO *watches him go.*

SANCHO: And if my Isle's no more real than those giants —

He shakes his head to get the thought out of it.

No, no! No, no, no! They're giants, they're giants. They're windmills . . . They're giants, they're giants.

He watches as hoofbeats sound.

Twenty yards . . . ten yards . . .

There is a great crash offstage. SANCHO *winces and groans.*

(*To his ass.*) Come on, my pearl. Let's pick up the pieces.

SCENE SEVEN

The courtyard of Don Quixote's house. The PRIEST *and* NICH-OLAS *are standing outside the house. On the ground is a pile of books. The* PRIEST *is reading one of them. The* BARBER *has one in each hand, closed, and is laboriously reading the titles.*

NICHOLAS: 'The History of Amadis the valiant Knight of Gaul. Book One.'

PRIEST (*without looking up from his book*): To the fire.

NICHOLAS: 'The History of Amadis of Gaul, Book Two'.

PRIEST (*as before*): To the fire.

    Two more books come flying through the window. NICHOLAS *picks them up.*

NICHOLAS: 'Amadis of Gaul, Book Three and Book Four'.

    The PRIEST *is engrossed in his book.*

Fire.

    More books come through the window.

'The Mirror of Chivalries'.

PRIEST (*preoccupied*): Fire.

NICHOLAS: Amadis of Gaul, Book Five.

PRIEST
       } Fire.
NICHOLAS

NICHOLAS: 'History of the Famous Knight Turante the White'.

PRIEST (*under his breath*): Fire.

NICHOLAS: 'Son of Amadis of Gaul'.

> *He looks up at the* PRIEST, *but he is too engrossed.*

Like father, like son.

> *He throws it with the rest.*

HOUSEKEEPER (*from inside*): That's the lot.

NICHOLAS: That's the lot. Reverend!

PRIEST: What say you, Sir Knight?

> *He draws an imaginary sword.*

I mean, erm – did you say something?

NICHOLAS: That's the lot of the chivalries.

PRIEST: Good. Let them all be burned. (*He returns to his book.*)

NICHOLAS: Do you think you ought to be reading that?

PRIEST: Hm? Why?

NICHOLAS: D'you think it's wise to read it, seeing as it's such a bad influence?

PRIEST: On others, friend. Not on me, naturally. Always on others. Still, I've had enough of it. Pernicious stuff. I'll take it home and finish it later.

> *The* NIECE *and the* STUDENT *come into the courtyard from outside. The* NIECE *is almost in tears.*

NIECE: There, you see? All your talk about leaving him alone to do what he likes —

STUDENT: I didn't say quite that. It's a question of the freedom of the individual —

NIECE: Well this is what it's come to! He's making himself a laughing stock!

PRIEST: Is there more news?

STUDENT: We met some merchants. They told us some cock-and-bull story ...

> *The* HOUSEKEEPER *comes out of the house.*

NIECE: They said they were set upon by a lunatic. A lunatic! (*She cries.*)

NICHOLAS: Sounds like our bird. What happened?

NIECE: The same as last time. He stood in their path and tried to make them admit that his lady Dulcinea, whoever she is, is the fairest in the world. It's so humiliating . . .

STUDENT: You have to admire his spirit.

PRIEST: Spirit is a very dangerous commodity my son. You'd do better without it. So then?

NIECE: They quite rightly answered that they couldn't admit any such thing, not having seen the lady.

STUDENT: These merchants – all logic and no poetry.

NIECE: So then he put his lance down, put spurs to his horse and charged at them.

HOUSEKEEPER: God in heaven!

The PRIEST *shakes his head sadly.*

NICHOLAS: Was any one hurt I hope? I mean, I hope no-one was hurt.

NIECE: No . . . (*She sobs.*) He fell off his horse before he got there. (*She cries.*)

NICHOLAS *sniggers behind his hand.*

STUDENT: Then they pummelled him there on the ground and rode on, the cowards.

NIECE: They're on their way to report it to the Holy Brotherhood.

NICHOLAS: And we know what'll happen if *they* catch up with him.

HOUSEKEEPER: To think he was always so respectable. Books! (*She kicks them.*)

The STUDENT *winces.*

PRIEST: This is what comes of losing one's sense of proportion and getting high-flown ideas. If only people would learn to leave all that to the Church. Well, friend Nicholas, I think the time has come for us to do our charitable duty.

NICHOLAS: Find him and lug him back?

PRIEST: *Persuade* him to come back.

He pats the NIECE's *hand.*

Never fear, my dear, we'll have your uncle back in the fold again.

NICHOLAS *pats the* HOUSEKEEPER's *hand.*

NICHOLAS: If we have to carry him by the ears.

PRIEST: Come, let's perfect our plan.

The PRIEST *and* NICHOLAS *go. The* HOUSEKEEPER *picks up some of the books.*

STUDENT: Where are you going with those?

HOUSEKEEPER: To the bonfire, where else?

She goes.

STUDENT: What tricks are those two up to, I wonder. I hope they don't . . .

NIECE: What?

STUDENT: Humiliate him.

NIECE: At least they're going to do something. All you do is talk. (*She goes angrily inside.*)

The STUDENT *looks at the books.*

STUDENT: They shouldn't treat books like that.

SCENE EIGHT

The road. SANCHO *and* DON QUIXOTE *are sitting eating their midday meal of bread, cheese, onions and wine which* SANCHO *is squirting into his mouth from a wineskin. He belches, wipes his mouth and sighs. He may be a little drunk.*

SANCHO: I've been thinking, Master; there's you, Don Quixote of La Mancha, the great and noble Knight; and there's me, Sancho Panza, a squat pot-bellied apology for a Squire that most Knights wouldn't give house-room to. But then I remember where it says: 'Blessed are the poor in spirit, blessed are the meek' and I begin to see some sense in it. Look at it this way: What do you need to make you happy? Damsels to rescue, giants to kill, wrongs to right, Knights to fight, not to mention your armour and your honour and your chivalry and all the rest of it. And with all that, you're not what I'd call a man at peace with himself.

DON QUIXOTE: True, Sancho. I'm not.

SANCHO: And now look at me. I'm sitting here, and I'm content. If everyone was as contented as I am now there'd be no trouble in the world and you'd be out of a job. And what did I need to put me in this state? I'll tell you: A bit of bread, a chunk of cheese, a skin of wine and an onion.

DON QUIXOTE: You could say as much for a beast of the field, Sancho.

SANCHO: That's true. I'm a beast first, and a man a long way second. When all's said and done, there's only one tyrant I find worth the fighting, and that's an empty belly.

DON QUIXOTE: Tell me, then, my contented friend: If I take out a coin and toss it away, will you leave it there?

He takes out a coin and makes as though to throw it, as if SANCHO *were a dog to run and fetch it.*

SANCHO *watches the coin plaintively, seeing his little castle of contentment crumbling.*

DON QUIXOTE *takes pity on him and throws him the coin.* SANCHO *catches it and examines it sadly.*

SANCHO: You're a clever man, your honour. I thought I was content, and you only had to show me this to prove I was wrong. It takes education to do that. There's only one thing I can say to that, and that's this. Ignorant idiots like me are not all that keen on the truth. We can't always afford it, so we use it like garlic, just enough and no more. By which I mean, there's times when educated men might keep their education to themselves and let us idiots go on fooling ourselves. As for this proof of yours, I'll keep it, but the devil take it. And now, by your leave, I'm going to sleep – where I *know* I'll be content. If you want to prove me out of that too, a kick in the ribs will do it; but I'd rather you didn't.

SANCHO *lies back and goes to sleep.*

DON QUIXOTE: Poor Sancho. Truth is bread, not garlic. If ever the time comes when my stomach for truth is as weak as yours, take me home and put me to bed, for I'll have had enough of life.

But what comes here?

The sound of hooves, the chattering of voices and the jingling of harness is heard.

Sancho! Sancho!

He nudges SANCHO *in the ribs.*

SANCHO: Oh, your honour, I *asked* you not to.

DON QUIXOTE: Wake up, Sancho. See what comes yonder.

SANCHO *looks.*

SANCHO: Oh, Lord . . .

DON QUIXOTE: If I mistake not this will be the most famous adventure ever seen; for those dark forms are certain wizards, carrying off in that coach some Princesses they have stolen.

SANCHO: This'll be a worse job than the windmills. Look, your worship, don't let the devil pull the wool over your eyes again. Your wizards there are Benedictine monks, with travelling masks to keep out the sun and dust. And your coachload of Princesses is a cartload of pigs. They're travelling together for safety, as well they might with people like us on the road.

DON QUIXOTE: Poor Sancho, why can you never face the truth?

SANCHO: But master —

DON QUIXOTE: Very well, think as you like. I shall keep the legitimate spoils of battle to myself.

SANCHO: Spoils of battle? (*He looks again.*) Spoils of . . . There *is* something wizardish about those monks.

DON QUIXOTE: Before the battle begins, heed what I say. You may defend yourself if set upon —

SANCHO: Thanks very much.

DON QUIXOTE: But as for helping me if I am attacked by

Knights, this you must not do, not being a Knight yourself,
So curb your natural impulses in that direction.

SANCHO: I'm glad you told me that. I'll bear it in mind. And
if there's any doubt whether it's a Knight which I can't
touch, or a base fellow which I can, I'll assume he's a Knight
out of politeness. As for defending myself, my usual strategy
is to confuse the enemy by running the other way.

DON QUIXOTE *has taken up his position on Rozinante,
lance at the ready.*

DON QUIXOTE: Monstrous and devilish crew! Release at
once the exalted Princesses or prepare to meet instant death
as a chastisement for your misdeeds!

SANCHO: Good for you, Master! That's got them in a sweat!

The procession enters and stops. At its head are two fat
MONKS *on their fat mules, with pasteboard masks covering their
faces; they are followed by their servants and other walking
travellers, and a cart.*

The MONKS *look at one another, then back at* DON QUIX-
OTE. *The* 1ST MONK *lifts his mask.*

1ST MONK: You are confusing us with someone else, Sir
Knight. We are two humble friars, as our servants here will
tell you.

The 2ND MONK *nods vigorously.*

DON QUIXOTE: Perfidious churls! Soft words will avail you
naught!

SANCHO: At 'em now, Master! Get their spoils!

DON QUIXOTE *lowers his lance and charges at the* 1ST
MONK, *who gives a little scream and falls off his mule.* DON
QUIXOTE *turns. The* 2ND MONK *makes off as fast as he can,
with* DON QUIXOTE *in pursuit. They both disappear offstage.*

SANCHO: Well done, your honour!

SANCHO runs up to the fallen 1ST MONK, takes hold of the money bag hanging at his waist and tries to pull it off. The servants and others, who have retreated at DON QUIXOTE's charge, approach.

SANCHO: Come, moneybag, come to your new master.

1ST SERVANT: What are you doing with our master's purse?

SANCHO: Money's the root of all evil, so I'm doing him a Christian service, by taking it upon myself. Which I've a right to do, and you can't touch me, it being the spoils of battle.

He attends again to the purse. The others close in on him silently. SANCHO looks up and sees them.

If you don't believe me, read your books of chivalry. I tell you it's spoils of battle. You can't touch me, my Knight says so. I'm base.

They look at one another silently. SANCHO grins. They jump on him. He disappears, yelling, under their flying fists.

The 1ST MONK gets up and dusts himself down. The others having finished with SANCHO, get up. SANCHO lies senseless. The 1ST MONK addresses him, after administering a kick.

1ST MONK: I have been taught to love my enemies. See, I turn the other cheek.

He does so, safely, SANCHO being unconscious. DON QUIXOTE appears, holding a handkerchief to his mouth. The 1ST MONK becomes aware of him.

The Holy Brotherhood will hear of this!

DON QUIXOTE approaches him and blows out a mouthful of teeth, his sword drawn. The 1ST MONK gives another little scream and hops offstage, one foot in the stirrup of his mule, as if scooting a bicycle. The others have retreated. DON QUIXOTE approaches the cart.

QUEEN MARGARET COLLEGE LIBRARY

DON QUIXOTE: Fear not, beauteous ladies, for your enchanters are fled and you are free. And if you would know the name of your deliverer, he is no other than Don Quixote of La Mancha, Knight Errant, adventurer, and captive only to the peerless Dona Dulcinea del Tobosa, whom I would have you visit, as a reward for my endeavours, to tell her of my deeds, and that I did them for her!

Grunts and whistles from the pigs in the cart.

How?! (*He looks inside the cart.*) Devils! You have transformed them into swine!!

The PIGMAN *appears, his sword in his hand, the others cautiously behind him.*

Is there no end to the evil in this world!

PIGMAN: Take the cart. I'll deal with this lunatic.

The others lead the cart away. DON QUIXOTE *and the* PIGMAN *engage in a furious swordfight around and over the body of* SANCHO, *characterised more by wild swipes and luck than by skill. Finally, after a particularly wild swing of his sword which spins* DON QUIXOTE *round like a top, the* PIGMAN *brings his sword down on* DON QUIXOTE's *helmet with a crash.* DON QUIXOTE *sinks to his knees.*

The PIGMAN *goes back a few steps for a run-up for the coup-de grace.* DON QUIXOTE *feels his broken helmet. He gives a terrible cry.*

DON QUIXOTE: Villain!!! You've broken my helmet!!

In a rage he leaps to his feet. The PIGMAN *terrified runs off.* DON QUIXOTE *goes after him a little, then stops, staggers, and comes back holding his head. He takes off his helmet, if it isn't off already, and looks at it sadly.*

This helmet was my Great-Grandfather's.

SANCHO *groans.*

Sancho, are you hurt?

SANCHO: No, your honour, I just thought I'd have a lie down. What happened?

DON QUIXOTE: We have just escaped from the power of the world's greatest sorcerers. Those Princesses, Sancho —

SANCHO: What Princesses?

DON QUIXOTE: The Princesses you took to be pigs – they were indeed pigs, transformed from Princesses.

SANCHO groans, puts his head in his hands and sobs.

What ails you?

SANCHO: I'm mixed up, that's what ails me. I'm black and blue, and I'm confused. (*He gets up, groaning and feeling his bruises.*) Where's my ass?

DON QUIXOTE: What do you want with your ass?

SANCHO: Comfort. Sympathy. Because she's an ass, and knows what it is to be beaten. (*He goes to her and rests his head against her neck, his arms round her.*) And security. Because whatever else I don't know, I do know she's not a castle, nor a giant, nor a bechanted Princess, but my own dear Dapple. (*He caresses her.*)

DON QUIXOTE: They broke my helmet, Sancho.

SANCHO: That's terrible. My bones, they're nothing, what are bones? But your honour's helmet, that's terrible. Your honour . . .

But DON QUIXOTE is examining the helmet sadly.

Master . . .

DON QUIXOTE looks up.

Give me my Isle. You must have won an Isle in that last battle. Give me the Isle you promised me and let me go and govern it, cos I've had enough . . .

DON QUIXOTE: I won no Isle, Sancho. Not that time . . .

Pause. SANCHO *shrugs.*

SANCHO: I didn't think you did. (*He gets painfully on to his ass.*) Let's go, Master; let's find the nearest church and hide ourselves a bit, before the Holy Brotherhood catch up with us.

DON QUIXOTE: Have you ever read in the chivalries of a Knight being arrested?

SANCHO: I can't *read*. Anyway, I'm not like you, always thinking about other people. I'm an ordinary base knave, and I was thinking about myself. And don't tell me no-one can touch a Knight's Squire, because I know they can.

DON QUIXOTE: Ah, Sancho, I'd give much for a draught of that miraculous balsam now.

SANCHO: Speak for yourself. But what do *you* want it for? You got off pretty light as far as I can see.

DON QUIXOTE: That wizard I chased hurled a rock at me.

SANCHO: Say a thunderbolt. If he was a wizard, have him throw a thunderbolt.

DON QUIXOTE: Whatever it was, I fear it took most of my teeth with it. See.

DON QUIXOTE *goes to* SANCHO *and opens his mouth.*

SANCHO: Aiee . . . Now there's a battlefield.

SANCHO *puts his fingers in* DON QUIXOTE's *mouth and he feels around.*

One . . . two . . . three . . . that's five cutters . . . three grinders . . . and a dogtooth. (*He shakes his head.*)

DON QUIXOTE: Gone?

SANCHO: Left. Does it hurt?

DON QUIXOTE: Knights do not voice their pain.

SANCHO: But does it hurt!

DON QUIXOTE: Let me say that I would fain rest a while

before we ride on, for I would . . . (*He holds his jaw gently.*) not . . . be . . . jolted . . .

SANCHO *holds his own jaw in sympathy.*

SANCHO: Oh, my poor master . . . Oh, your honour, how did you ever pick yourself such a *base – selfish – clod* of a squire? You're in agony. Lie down, master, and sleep the pain off. I'll keep watch.

DON QUIXOTE: I will lie down. (*He does so.*) As for sleep, I'll not manage that . .

SANCHO: Yes, you will. Look, I'll tell you a story. I've a special tale for sending one to sleep, it never fails, I had it from my mother, and she from her mother, and so it goes back to Adam and Eve for all I know. It's an old tale. Lie back, Master, and rest, and I'll tell it. (*He clears his throat.*) In the village of Estremadura, or one not far from it, there was a shepherd – that is, a goatherd, for he kept goats. Now this shepherd or goatherd, as the story goes, was called Lope Ruiz, and this Lope Ruiz fell in love with a shepherdess who was called Torralva, and this shepherdess called Torralva was daughter to a rich farmer, and this rich farmer —

DON QUIXOTE: If you repeat everything twice you'll not be finished in a fortnight.

SANCHO: I'm sorry, Master, but that's how they tell tales in my parts, and it's the only way I know. You can't teach an old dog new tricks; in a strange house a wise man's a fool and when in Rome it's best to —

DON QUIXOTE: Tell it as you please.

SANCHO: This shepherd fell in love with Torralva, a very buxom, mannish wench. —

DON QUIXOTE: Mannish?

SANCHO: Little moustaches she had, the darling, I can see her now.

DON QUIXOTE: You knew her?

SANCHO: No, no, I never met her, it was before my time. So, days came and days went, and the devil, ever on the look-out, so contrived it that the shepherd's love was all turned to hate, why, no-one knew unless it was the devil himself as I said. And finally this shepherd hated so much the one he loved that he decided to go where his eye would never again see her – He had only the one eye, I forgot to tell you. While Torralva, when she found herself jilted by Lope, fell to loving him ten times more than before.

DON QUIXOTE: Such are women. They love those that hate them and hate those that love them.

SANCHO: As you say, I wouldn't know. Well, the shepherd took the road across the plains of Estremadura, driving his sheep before him —

DON QUIXOTE: I thought they were goats.

SANCHO: Goats they are. Bound for the Kingdom of Portugal. And Torralva, when she heard of it, followed after. So, when Lope came to the river which was all swollen with the rains, all he wanted was to get across there as soon as he could, seeing Torralva coming up behind in her bare feet, ready to weep and moan and give him a devil of a time. But never a boat could be found. Till he saw a fisherman, and this fisherman – There, I've done it again. I can't help it, you see.

DON QUIXOTE: Just go on.

SANCHO: This fisherman had a boat so small it could take no more than one man and one goat. But he arranged for the fisherman to take him and his three hundred goats across

the river. So, the fisherman got in the boat, and took a goat,
and carried over the goat, and came back. And then he took
another goat, and carried over the goat, and came back.
And then he took another goat, and carried over the goat,
and came back. And then he took another goat, and carried
– If your honour would keep count of the goats we'll get it
done quicker between the two of us, for I'm no great shakes
at counting. And then he took another goat —

DON QUIXOTE: Can we not reckon them already over?
and go on from there?

SANCHO: How can we do that, master, if we haven't counted
them over? We'd be like to leave one or two on the wrong
side. And I might add it's no easy matter getting these goats
over, the banks being all slippery with mud. But never
mind that, we'll go on. How many goats are over?

DON QUIXOTE: How the devil do I know?

SANCHO: Well I'm damned if I do. So we'll just have to start
again with the first. And if you keep the score this time as I
said, we'll get the job done sooner. The fisherman took a
goat, and carried over the goat, and came back. Then he
took a goat, and carried over the goat, and came back.
Then he took a goat, and carried over the goat, and came
back. Then he took a goat . . .

   SANCHO *continues. His voice gets slower. Sitting astride his
ass, he sleeps.*

DON QUIXOTE: Sancho . . .?

   No answer. DON QUIXOTE *closes his eyes. He too sleeps.
The* 1ST BANDIT *appears. He comes on stealthily, makes sure
the two are asleep, and beckons. The* 2ND BANDIT *enters. The*
2ND BANDIT *examines Rozinante. He looks inquiringly at the*
1ST BANDIT *and points to Rozinante. The* 1ST BANDIT *shakes*

his head and points to SANCHO's *ass. The* 2ND BANDIT *nods.*
1ST BANDIT *points to an overhanging bough above* SANCHO's
head. The 2ND BANDIT *goes off, while the* 1ST BANDIT
unbuckles Dapple's saddle-girths. The 2ND BANDIT *comes back
with a length of rope, to one end of which are attached a number of
hooks. He throws the other end of the rope over the bough. The*
1ST BANDIT *hooks on the saddle. Both* BANDITS *haul on the
other end, and* SANCHO *is raised an inch from his ass. They tie
the rope to a low branch or root. The* 1ST BANDIT *takes out a
carrot which he holds in front of the ass. The ass advances and
follows him offstage. The* 2ND BANDIT *takes the panniers
attached to the saddle, and also makes off.*

A pause. SANCHO *wakes up. He snorts, groans, feels his
bruises.*

SANCHO: Now it's raining . . . And I ache all over . . . Well,
now, Sancho, enough bellyaching. Copy your valiant
master for a change. Look on the bright side, if you can find
one. Let's see – rain's good for the crops . . . As for your
aching bones, at least you've still got a mouthful of teeth.
What's more, you've got your dear Dapple. Life's not so
bad . . .

*He pats the ass's neck, or tries to. He feels around frantically,
then looks down, to see himself suspended in mid-air. He gives a
terrible cry of anguish, and topples out of the saddle on to the
ground, where he continues to cry out, waking* DON QUIXOTE
who jumps to his feet waving his sword.

DON QUIXOTE: What is it! Are you bewitched?

SANCHO: Worse! Robbed! They've stolen my ass from under
me!

DON QUIXOTE: A very powerful charm, to spirit an ass
from under your weight.

SANCHO: Charm nothing! Look! (*He waves at the rope and saddle.*)

DON QUIXOTE: Most ingenious. T'would be worth the loss of an ass to have seen that operation.

SANCHO: Oh would it! I'm glad of that! I'll bear that in mind!

DON QUIXOTE: Come, Sancho, what's an ass after all?

SANCHO: Nothing to you, I daresay. But to me, I'll tell you what she was. She was born in my own home; she played with my children; she carried my burdens; she earned my living; she was my child, my friend – my bit of property. (*He cries.*)

DON QUIXOTE: Come now, Sancho. Listen: At home I have five ass-foals. I'll give you two of them.

    SANCHO *looks up, sobbing.*

Three.

    SANCHO *stops sobbing, sniffs, gets up, wipes his nose.*

SANCHO: Three ass-foals?

    DON QUIXOTE *nods.*

You'll write it down to make it official?

DON QUIXOTE: If you wish.

SANCHO: Well, then . . .

    He clears his throat and wipes his eyes. Then he calls offstage to his absent ass.

Short tears, Dapple. That's the way it is. Don't think too bad of me. Three asses for one ass. I can't afford sentiment . . . Just don't let them beat you . . .

    He turns to DON QUIXOTE.

Enough of that. Now let's forget it. Sancho's got a bargain for once. I think. Let's move on, Master, for suddenly I hate this place.

E

He begins to untie the rope and saddle. DON QUIXOTE *looks offstage, where there is the sound of hooves and a man singing.*

DON QUIXOTE: Wait, Sancho! Here comes someone to reverse our fortunes.

SANCHO *looks.*

SANCHO: A travelling barber? To reverse our fortunes? Master, if all I needed was a beard trim —

DON QUIXOTE: That is no barber.

SANCHO: Oh, *Master* ... (*He shakes his head.*) The *giants* ... The *castle* ... The *wizards* ...

DON QUIXOTE: I don't follow your drift. What have they to do with yonder Knight?

SANCHO: Nothing, nothing ... (*He looks at the sky.*) It's not a travelling barber, who's put his basin on his head to keep off the rain ... It's a *Knight* ... with a *helmet* ...

DON QUIXOTE: *The* helmet. If I mistake not, the helmet worn by yon Knight on his dappled steed is no other than that fabled golden helm of Mambrino, the most coveted in the world.

SANCHO *nods, past disagreeing.*

Draw aside now, and see how I shall take it from him.

SANCHO: That I'll do. As for what comes out of it , I'm past meddling.

SANCHO *withdraws behind the tree,* DON QUIXOTE *mounts Rozinante, takes up his lance and goes offstage, the opposite side from the approaching barber. The* BARBER *enters, in good spirits in spite of the rain. He sees* SANCHO *behind the tree and stops singing.*

BARBER: Good day to you, friend.

SANCHO: Oh, is it? Mark what I say then: Let it be what it will, it's none of my business.

BARBER: What?

    DON QUIXOTE *appears.*

DON QUIXOTE: Defend yourself, vile caitiff creature, or render up of your own will that which by all right is mine!

    So saying, he puts spurs to Rozinante and charges. The BARBER *yelps, slides off his ass and runs, leaving both ass and basin.*

A wise man. Pick up the helmet, Sancho.

    SANCHO *comes from behind the tree, picks up the basin and looks at it.*

SANCHO: It's a good basin. (*He raps it with his knuckles.*) Solid brass. Worth a real of anyone's money.

    He hands it to DON QUIXOTE *with a sour expression.* DON QUIXOTE *puts it on, turning it to find the visor.*

DON QUIXOTE: But no vizor.

SANCHO: They don't often put 'em on barbers' basins.

DON QUIXOTE: Truly it is like a basin.

SANCHO: It is. I've never seen a basin so like a basin.

DON QUIXOTE: This is what I think has happened. This enchanted helmet —

    SANCHO *strikes his head.*

— has fallen into the hands of some smith ignorant of its magic, who melted the vizor half down for its gold, and fashioned *this* half into a barber's basin. But it matters not, the magic is still in it.

    DON QUIXOTE *examines it again.* SANCHO *turns away in disgust; on the turn, his eye lights on the ass. He does a double-take. He looks in the direction taken by the* BARBER, *looks at the ass, at* DON QUIXOTE, *at the* BARBER, *at himself, at the ass, He strokes his chin.*

SANCHO: Master . . .

DON QUIXOTE (*looking at the helmet*): The steed, of course, you may keep as spoils of battle.

SANCHO's face breaks into a smile.

SANCHO: And not a soul in sight to pummel me for it!

He advances cautiously on the ass, afraid it might disappear, then catches its bridle. He laughs with glee.

SANCHO: *Four* asses now. Three paper ones and one flesh. Oh, I'm a rogue! Tell me, your honour, did you ever hear of any rogue of a merchant who multiplied his stock by four in as many minutes! Oh, he's a – (*He looks.*) She's a good ass. A well-kept ass. Let's have a look under the saddle . . . (*He takes it off.*) Look not a rib showing. This ass has lived on the fat of the land. Good-natured too; aren't you, my beauty, my darling? This ass has a loving disposition, I can tell you that. Women are a mystery to me, but asses I can read like a book. This is an ass in a million. I pity that barber, he must have doted on her. See how well he kept her. Fed her with titbits from his own dinner, petted her and combed her and told her his troubles; and sang songs to her as they travelled, to while away the journey. And now she's gone. And he's sitting behind a rock somewhere, I daresay, in the rain, without a soul for company, minus his basin, minus his ass, the only friend he had in the world . . .

He is now blubbering freely. He looks at the ass, then yells at it. Traitor! Wretch! Temptress! Is there no pity left in the world, that you'd leave your master after all he's done for you, and just when he needs you most, having just had his ass stolen by some vile, heartless, stinking knave! Go, go back to your master, you brazen bitch, you slut! Go back, you bag of bones! Go back! Go back!

He beats her off the stage, and cries.

DON QUIXOTE: I'm beginning to wonder if you've taken leave of your wits. Are you to weep at every ass you see? You'd do well to model yourself on Knights errrant such as me. Do I weep at misfortune? No. Do I worry over my possessions? No. Hungry or thirsty, weary or wounded, I make no complaint. My satisfaction is not of the body but of the spirit; my most cherished possession the thought that throughout the land the poor and the oppressed are thinking of me with gratitude for the wrongs I have righted and the loads I have lifted from their backs. Fie on you, Sancho; copy me, though you be only a Squire.

The SHEPHERD LAD *enters.*

And see – as if sent from Heaven to prove my point. Do you remember me, boy?

LAD: Do I not!

DON QUIXOTE: Where are you off to now lad?

LAD: Running away, what d'you think?

DON QUIXOTE: What! After I made your master pay you! Ungrateful wretch, would you undo all the good I did?

LAD: If only I could! (*He turns to* SANCHO.)

He paid me all right! When he got me home he gave me the biggest beating I've had in my life, and I've had some. He beat me for myself, then he beat me for him. That's how he paid me, and he's promised me the same wage again next week. So I'm off. And you might tell that master of yours in future to keep his help for them as is strong enough for it, and for the rest, to mind his own business

The LAD *leaves.* DON QUIXOTE *watches him go, full of consternation.*

DON QUIXOTE: There must be some mistake . . . I don't understand . . .

SANCHO: Don't you? Then let me explain.

He stands looking at DON QUIXOTE's *crestfallen figure, trying to avoid pitying him.*

The devil take it! The devil take it all! The devil take all Knights and all castles, and the devil take wandering about this lousy world on kicks and empty bellies, and the devil take doing good and the devil take chilvary! And the devil take you for separating me from my wife and my home and my ass for the sake of an Isle when I don't even know what an Isle is, and the devil take me for being a fool enough to be taken in by it all!

He stops. DON QUIXOTE *falls to his knees, utterly dejected.* SANCHO *looks at him for a moment and shakes his head.*

Take no notice of me, Master. (*He goes up to him.*) Take no notice . . .

SCENE NINE

Outside the Inn. SANCHO *approaches, riding Rozinante. He stops, looks at the Inn, dismounts, looks at the audience, looks at Rozinante and rubs his backside.*

SANCHO: Bonebag . . . How your master manages on you I don't know. He hasn't got my upholstery. (*He looks at the Inn again.*) I'm hot; I'm tired; I'm thirsty; I've nothing in my belly but road-dust: and where do I find myself? Outside that same plaguey Inn where they tormented me. (*He sniffs.*) Stew . . . Beef stew with lots of onions . . . 'Go in and eat, fool!' cries my belly. 'Stay outside, you idiot!' says my back. (*He hesitates.*) It's a fine thing when your own body has arguments with itself.

He hears the INNKEEPER'S *voice yelling at* MARIA.

Devil take the place! And belly, stop bellyaching. You can't get any emptier. (*So saying, he puts a foot in the stirrup to ride on.*)

At this moment the PRIEST *and* NICHOLAS *the barber come out of the Inn.*

NICHOLAS: Hey, fellow!

SANCHO *hides behind Rozinante.*

SANCHO: Who fellows me? They can fill their lousy blanket with someone else. There's no fellow here! Just the horse! *Walk, you bone-bag . . .*

NICHOLAS: A horse with six legs, is it? (*He runs out and seizes the bridle.*) What's the hurry, Master Sancho? Why so unsociable? Don't you recognise Nicholas the barber?

SANCHO: No haircut today, thank you.

> SANCHO *tries to go on.* NICHOLAS *prevents him, the* PRIEST *arrives.*

PRIEST: I've not seen you at Mass of late, Sancho Panza.

SANCHO: Reverend! You're a long way from your parish.

PRIEST: You too, Sancho.

SANCHO: I've been on a trip.

PRIEST: So I've heard. Without even kissing your spouse goodbye.

SANCHO: I'm a simple Christian, Reverend, I don't go in much for that kind of thing. And now I'll be getting on my way.

PRIEST: Not so fast. Where is Senor Quixada?

SANCHO: Who?

NICHOLAS: Don't play about with us, fellow.

SANCHO: If it's Don Quixote you mean, he's – back there. (*He gives a vague wave of his hand to take in half the countryside.*)

PRIEST: Come, it won't do. Where is your master and what is he doing?

> SANCHO *twists and turns.*

SANCHO: With all respect, reverend, I'd tell you if I could, but I'm sworn not to, and I can't break my oath not for all the eyes in my head; for that's a sin, and you wouldn't want it, would you? All I can say is this: he's out there; he's busy with a certain – business, and doesn't want any help with it, may God rest him.

PRIEST: Amen.

SANCHO: And amen to your amen, reverend.

NICHOLAS: Villain!

SANCHO: What?

NICHOLAS: I'll tell you what his business is: it's lying out there with his life's blood running out. And why can't you tell us? Because it's you did it, and then stole his horse and there it is for proof, you rogue!

SANCHO: Rogue yourself! That's all lies, reverend. He's got blood on the brain, through seeing so much of it shaving his clients.

PRIEST: If you don't tell us the truth, Sancho, we must believe the worst.

SANCHO: All right. I'll tell you. He's at penance.

PRIEST: At what?

SANCHO: He's doing penitence in the wilderness.

PRIEST: For what sin?

SANCHO: For no sin; for a lady. It's chilvary so I don't expect to make sense of it. All I know is, he's out there now leaping about naked and cracking rocks with his head – please God it's not the other way about – and scratching out poems in the sand while he gets his breath back. He wanted me to watch him. 'Wait while I strip off,' he said, 'And you can watch me hop about like a mad thing and beat my head against the rocks, like they do in the chilvaries. Then you can tell my Lady Dulcinea at first hand what I done.' For pity's sake sir, I said, do it when I've gone and I'll use my imagination, for I don't want to weep any more. I'm too soft-hearted . . . So I'm on my way to the lady now with a letter, and I'm to tell her he'll carry on these capers till she makes him fair answer. So I'd best be on my way.

NICHOLAS: A likely tale!

PRIEST: Which lady is this?

SANCHO: I told you, the Lady Dulcinea, otherwise known as Aldonza Lorenzo of El Toboso.

NICHOLAS *hoots with laughter.*

NICHOLAS: That Aldonza? The big one? The Lady what? Ho ho.

PRIEST: It's a sad business.

NICHOLAS: Oh, a crying shame. This Lady Dulcinea's the best cattle-caller in the district. What a voice! And as strong as a horse. She once had a wrestling match with the blacksmith, reverend, for a bet —

PRIEST: Yes, yes. And you're taking her a letter?

SANCHO: On a bit of paper. I'm to get it copied out fair the first educated man I come across, leaving aside apothecaries.

PRIEST: Why leaving aside apothecaries?

SANCHO: Because Don Quixote says there's no-one on earth can read your apothecary's writing, unless it's another apothecary.

PRIEST: I'll copy it out for you, Sancho. Give me the letter.

SANCHO: Here it is, reverend . . .

He searches about him, more and more frantically. His mouth drops open in utter consternation. Then he begins to beat himself wildly.

PRIEST: Is he ill?

SANCHO: What should I be, when I lose three ass-foals before I even set eyes on them! Idiot!

NICHOLAS: He's as mad as his master.

PRIEST: What ass-foals, Sancho?

SANCHO: Three that my Knight promised me, since I had mine stolen from under me. It was writ on the back of that paper. And I've lost the lot!

PRIEST: Console yourself; that paper was worthless.

SANCHO: Worthless?

PRIEST: These things have to be done in the proper manner; on parchment, through a notary, with seals and witnesses; not on the back of a love-letter.

  SANCHO *groans.*

But don't worry, I'll press him to make them over to you properly.

SANCHO: You will? You'll press him?

PRIEST: As soon as I see him. (*With a glance at* NICHOLAS.)

SANCHO: Well then, that's not so bad. Then there's nothing lost, for I have the letter by heart; he read it out to me. And a fine flowing thing it was too, enough to wring the heart of the devil himself.

  The PRIEST *crosses himself.*

NICHOLAS: Let's hear it, then; recite it out.

SANCHO: Shall I?

PRIEST: Yes.

SANCHO: Right. Er . . .

  SANCHO *scratches his head, pulls his nose, stands on one leg, looks to the sky, chews his finger, etc.*

Well, I'll get the start of it out first, and it might drag the rest with it. 'Your –'. No. 'His –'. No. Wait! I've got it. 'Crude and Salted Lady —'

  NICHOLAS *creases.*

Yes, it caught *my* fancy, that crude and salted.

PRIEST: Are you sure it wasn't cruel and exalted?

  SANCHO *looks at him for a moment.*

SANCHO: That's good too. Then it goes on: 'The disparaging and sleepless Knight begs for clementines —'

PRIEST: Desperate, was it, or despairing, and begs for clemency?

SANCHO: Reverend, if you're going to stop me when I'm in full spate I'll lose the lot. '—begs for clemen — whatever it was, from that exhausted, naughty and beauteic ungrate Dulcinea del Toboso.

NICHOLAS (*weakly*): Beauteic ungrate . . .

SANCHO: Something something . . . Then there's a 'thankless fair!' and then it goes scrambling on, 'If that your—' something or other, and there's an anguish and a disdain though I wouldn't swear which comes first; and after that it's not quite so firm in my mind. But I've got the other end of it as well, so the middle must still be safe in there. It ends: 'Yours till death, the Knight of the Woeful Continence' which is what he's pleased to call himself.

NICHOLAS *is beating the ground.*

PRIEST: Do you mean countenance?

SANCHO: I don't mean anything, reverend, it's all Dutch to me, As for Don Quixote, if the lady takes pity on one of the two I daresay he'll be content, be it his countenance or his continence. What's up with this – *fellow*?

PRIEST: Tell me, Sancho, do you want the best for your master?

SANCHO: I do.

PRIEST: So do I. Which is why we are here. Sancho, your master has fallen into error.

SANCHO: How's that, reverend?

PRIEST: Why, setting himself up to right the world's wrongs – taking the law into his own hands; we have an institution for that purpose.

SANCHO: The Holy Brotherhood.

PRIEST: Exactly. What would *you* do, if you were a shepherd and someone took it upon himself to look after your sheep?

SANCHO: Stay in bed.

PRIEST: I'm saying it would be best if your master could be persuaded to return to his house and live again as a law-abiding man.

SANCHO: There's a snag there.

PRIEST: What?

SANCHO: If he goes home, how will I ever get the Isle he promised me?

The PRIEST *and* NICHOLAS *exchange glances.*

NICHOLAS: What would you do with an Isle?

SANCHO: Govern it, what else do you do with an Isle? Shave it?

NICHOLAS: You govern an Isle! That I'd like to see!

SANCHO: Is it right for this face-butcher to call my master a liar?

NICHOLAS: Reverend, would you stop this fellow insulting my profession. (*To* SANCHO.) I'm the best barber in the district!

SANCHO: You're the only barber in the district. You killed the other one shaving him.

NICHOLAS: I'll get you in my chair one of these days, Master Squire and then —

PRIEST: Hush, Nicholas. Sancho, your master has no Isle to give you.

SANCHO: Not yet he hasn't. But as soon as he wins a kingdom for himself he'll give me one.

PRIEST: A kingdom?

SANCHO: He's only just missed one two or three times already by the skin of his teeth. But it's not for want of trying he's not quite done it yet, nor for the want of valour! It's the bechantment that's done him in the eye every time, nothing but that, and I won't have anyone say any different.

NICHOLAS *points to his head behind* SANCHO's *back.*

PRIEST: Calm yourself, Sancho. Well at least you want Don Quixote to leave this place he's immured himself in, don't you?

SANCHO: I do. And before he bashes his brains out if possible.

PRIEST: But I fear your task is hopeless. By the time you find this Aldonza, give your message, wait for her answer and return to your master, he'll surely be a corpse.

SANCHO: Don't say that, reverend!

PRIEST: I only say what I think. I know what I'd do in your place . . .

SANCHO: What's that?

PRIEST: No, you must do as *you* think fit . . .

SANCHO: Reverend, if it's good enough for you it's good enough for me.

PRIEST: Then what *I'd* do would be to go straight back to Don Quixote, tell him I'd given her the letter, that she was overjoyed to hear from him and wished only that he would fly straight home where she will be waiting.

SANCHO: That sounds good; but how can I tell him all that if I haven't seen the lady?

The PRIEST *and* NICHOLAS *sigh at each other.*

PRIEST: Sancho, you *say* you've seen her; you *say* you have a message from her . . .

SANCHO: When I haven't.

PRIEST: Exactly.

SANCHO: Then how do I get the message?

PRIEST: You *make it up*, Sancho!

SANCHO *thinks. Light dawns*

SANCHO: Ah . . . ! Is that honest?

NICHOLAS: Now would your Priest ask you to do a dishonest thing?

SANCHO: No. That's logical . . . In that case I'm in agreement with that, reverend. I'll do it, and save my feet and his skull at the same time.

PRIEST: Very wise. A brilliant idea of yours, Sancho.

SANCHO: Of mine . . . ?

PRIEST: We can go home again, Nicholas; our minds are at rest; Don Quixote is safe in Sancho's hands, that's clear.

NICHOLAS: Eh? But reverend —

The PRIEST *gives him a shove.*

PRIEST: Come, then, we'll all eat at the Inn and then be on about our business. (*He propels* NICHOLAS *towards the Inn.*) (*s.v*) We'll follow him. And if Dulcinea's message doesn't do the trick, our plan will.

NICHOLAS: Say no more. (*To* SANCHO.) One thing's for sure if you tell this message as well as you told the other, it'll cure your master of his melancholy. Ho, ho.

PRIEST: Are you coming to eat, Sancho? I'll pay.

SANCHO: In that case, if you'd have your fellow there bring me something out. Just a bowl or two of that stew will do, no fish if you please. I'd come in, but the horse has taken a hatred to the place; I think she must have had a beating there.

SCENE TEN

The desert. DON QUIXOTE *sits alone, dressed but without his armour. He is a sorry sight. He sings to himself, perhaps to an offstage guitar, a song he has just composed, and which he has been scratching out in the dust.*

DON QUIXOTE: 'Though desolate this spot
And bare of all things growing,
Sun merciless and hot
And dusty dust a-blowing,
Vacate it he would not;
For there could never be a
More meet and fitting plot
For doleful Don Quixote
To weep for Dulcine – a.
               Del Toboso.

'This is the perfect spot
True lover for to mourn his
Wretched and thankless lot
And wish he never born is — was;
Though wots he not a jot
Why he should weep such te-ars
To fill an outsize pot.
O, luckless Don Quixote,
Who weeps for Dulcine – a.
               Del Toboso.'

SANCHO *appears, on foot.*

SANCHO: Master . . .

DON QUIXOTE *engrossed in his melancholy, seems not to hear him.*

Your honour – Don Quixote – it's me – your Sancho.

DON QUIXOTE *looks up.*

DON QUIXOTE: I've missed you, Sancho.

SANCHO *runs to him and embraces him.*

SANCHO: I've missed you, Master, may God help me. Oh, but you're thinner than ever. What have you been eating?

DON QUIXOTE: Roots and berries. Penance-food.

SANCHO: Roots and berries . . . Well, your honour's head's in one piece anyway.

DON QUIXOTE: I have been melancholy, Sancho.

SANCHO: I'll cheer you up, Master, I'm famous for my comical tales, I'll tell you some on the way. And if I don't go sticking the tail of one tale on to the head of another which is a habit I fall into, you'll laugh yourself sick.

DON QUIXOTE: Later, Sancho. What news have you for me?

SANCHO: You mean with regard to the lady.

DON QUIXOTE: Yes, yes.

SANCHO: Now there's a lady, your honour, you did well to pick that one to journey off from. There's not many women like that left. Did you know about this wrestling match she had with the blacksmith for a bet, the winner to take as much wine as he could hold, or she as it turned out, and how she broke his arm winning it? And how to get his own back, this blacksmith —

DON QUIXOTE: Sancho! What news do you have?

SANCHO: Any amount, Master. As much as you like, in fact, and as for content, whatever takes your fancy.

DON QUIXOTE: First, is she well?

SANCHO: As far as I know.

DON QUIXOTE: As far as you know? How did she look? How was her colour? Was she pale?

SANCHO: Flesh-coloured, your honour.

DON QUIXOTE: And how did she take the letter?

SANCHO: How? Er – between her teeth. She was plucking a goose at the time.

DON QUIXOTE: I mean how did it affect her? Was she moved?

SANCHO: Ah, there you've hit it. I've never seen anyone moved as she was moved. 'From Don Quixote!' she screamed out between her teeth. 'From my Knight!' And you know what a voice she's got, they heard it in the next village I'm told, even with the letter still in her mouth. Then she jumped up, threw away the goose with such a force that they were still looking for it when I left, did a couple of somersaults and went hopping and screaming round the yard while the tears ran off the letter like rain off a roof.

All this he mimes as he tells it.

'Let me kiss the letter!' she cried, and for the next five minutes that's what she did, kissing it this way and that way till what with tears and spit she'd made a right mess of it; for she's a wet-lipped lady as you must have noticed.

DON QUIXOTE: Then she read it?

SANCHO: Then she read it. Oh, you should have seen her reading it! This way up, that way up, frontwards, backwards, and every new word she managed to make out she wept again. 'Disdain!' she cried, 'It says disdain!' And 'Here's a 'beauteic ungrate'! Let me swoon!' Which she did three or four times. The long and the short of it being that what with the energy she put into the reading of it, she lay exhausted for two hours after, unable to stir, though they bled her.

DON QUIXOTE: This is a good sign.

SANCHO: I thought it might be.

DON QUIXOTE: And she wrote you an answer?

SANCHO: That she did, five pages of it, and all in gold.

DON QUIXOTE: Then let me have it.

SANCHO: I should say, she *told* me an answer. 'Let me *tell* you the answer, she said, and you tell it to Don Quixote; because, one, I can't write to save my life; and, two, if I write it you'll lose it, and I won't have my letter lost when I've gone to such trouble writing it in gold!

DON QUIXOTE: Then tell me it. What did it say?

SANCHO: Ah . . . I tell you what, your honour: you tell me what you think she said, and I'll tell you if you're right.

DON QUIXOTE: I tell you? This is a strange way of receiving a letter.

SANCHO: It'll be all the better for it, believe me.

DON QUIXOTE: Then she began thus: 'To the noble, valorous and renowned Knight Don Quixote of La Mancha, in whom reside all virtues of honour, steadfastness, courage and fidelity, from that penitent and heartsick lady whose tears express what her pen cannot – greetings and felicitations.'

SANCHO: That's it, master, to a T. You've got every word. Go on, do.

DON QUIXOTE: 'Would that my pen could follow the desire of my heart and summon my brave champion at once to my side . . .'

SANCHO: 'To my side' was there; go on.

DON QUIXOTE: 'But it cannot be. For having demonstrated by feats of unexampled valour the proof of your love, there remains one task I would set you, one tyrant, the greatest of all, to overcome. Do this, and be mine.'

SANCHO: What tyrant's that, master?

DON QUIXOTE: She doesn't say.

SANCHO: Oh. That's a pity. For how will you know when you've done this task, if you don't know what it is?

DON QUIXOTE: We shall know, Sancho. For this will be an adventure so great, so perilous and so terrible that no other on earth has ever approached it.

SANCHO: And this is what your lady wants you to have a go at?

DON QUIXOTE: Such is the love she has for me.

SANCHO: Then love's a wondrous thing. Well, Master, you'd got that letter off pat, it's a miracle. In fact knowing the answer so well it was hardly worth sending for it, we could've done it all between us on the spot. You only missed one thing out.

DON QUIXOTE: What's that?

SANCHO: Where she said, for you to leave beating your head and come back to her at once.

DON QUIXOTE: She said that?

SANCHO: That's the one thing I'm sure of.

DON QUIXOTE: But how could she, when you say she's already told me to engage in this further adventure?

SANCHO *is stuck.*

SANCHO: Ah . . . You've got me in a corner there.

DON QUIXOTE: Come, Sancho, help me on with my armour. We must find this tyrant.

SANCHO: Yes, your honour . . . (*To himself.*) I'm not sure this has come out as it was meant to . . .

The PRIEST *enters. He is wearing a beard made out of an oxtail.*

PRIEST: Sir Knight!

DON QUIXOTE: Who comes here?

NICHOLAS *follows the* PRIEST *on. He is disguised as a woman.*

PRIEST: At him, then, Nicholas.

The PRIEST *gives* NICHOLAS *a push.* NICHOLAS, *tripping over his skirts, stumbles across the stage and falls on his knees at* DON QUIXOTE's *feet.*

DON QUIXOTE: Rise, beauteous damsel, for it is I should do homage to you.

NICHOLAS *looks round at the* PRIEST.

PRIEST: Go on.

NICHOLAS (*getting up*): Brave Knight, I shall not rise —

PRIEST: Kneel . . .

NICHOLAS: He told me to get up.

PRIEST: *Kneel* . . .

NICHOLAS *kneels again.*

NICHOLAS: Brave Knight, I shall not rise from this spot until you — what?

PRIEST: Pledge me your word.

NICHOLAS: Pledge me your word.

DON QUIXOTE: Word on what, fair lady?

NICHOLAS: Word on what?

The PRIEST *shows exasperation.*

Ah. Yes. That you will rid me of that giant that – wait a minute – ravishes my kingdom.

PRIEST: Ravages.

NICHOLAS: Ravages.

DON QUIXOTE: Which kingdom is this, Princess?

    NICHOLAS *puts his hand to his head.*

NICHOLAS: Don't tell me . . . Ah, yes. I am Princess Mico-
micona ruler of the mighty Kingdom Micomicon, which
lies yonder.

    He points. The PRIEST *swings his arm till it points in the
opposite direction.*

PRIEST: As you can see, Sir Knight, my mistress is out of her
wits – with grief. Many knights have tried to kill this giant
and paid for it with their lives. It is said that there is but one
man who could perhaps vanquish it.

DON QUIXOTE: Who is that?

PRIEST: The name escapes me; something like – Don Pickrope
or Don Thicksoap.

SANCHO: It couldn't be Don Quixote . .

NICHOLAS
             } That's the one!
PRIEST

SANCHO: That's you, Master!

DON QUIXOTE: Did you ever doubt it, Sancho? I am that
Don Quixote.

PRIEST: Grieve no more, Princess, for our search has been
rewarded.

NICHOLAS: Wondrous Heaven! You are the great Don
Quixote?

DON QUIXOTE: Rise, fair Princess, and lead me to your
kingdom; for your boon is granted. I vow to undertake no
other adventure, and neither to eat sleep nor wash till I have
smitten this giant into a thousand pieces.

NICHOLAS: Aaah . . . !

DON QUIXOTE: Lead on, Princess; I'll follow.

The PRIEST *and* NICHOLAS *shake hands and withdraw.*

DON QUIXOTE *finishes putting his armour on.*

Our luck has turned, Sancho; this can only be the work of Providence. For this surely is that very task set me by Dulcinea, this that so many Knights have perished attempting.

SANCHO: I'm glad to hear it. All I can say is, your lady and Providence are a couple of hard taskmasters.

DON QUIXOTE: Cheer up, Sancho. Are you not glad to see me in good spirits at last?

SANCHO: I am. I just hope they stay so.

DON QUIXOTE: They will. For at last I have a task worthy of my mettle. As for you, this time you shall get your Isle. This time surely.

DON QUIXOTE *follows the other two off.*

SANCHO: That's good news . . . My Isle . . . I should be skipping now. Why am I not . . .? Pessimist! Idiot! (*He begins to follow the others; stops.*) But something smells to me; and it's not stinking fish. (*He goes.*)

SCENE ELEVEN

*The yard of the Inn. The sun is setting. Music and commotion is
heard off, and a little procession enters the yard: Master* PETER,
the Puppeteer, with drums or timbrels; the MUSICIANS *playing,
the Puppeteer's* BOY *dragging behind him the stage cart; a* BEAR
*on a chain; etc. Following the procession come villagers in festive
dress, perhaps with masks.* PETER *stops, silences the Musicians
with a roll on the drums, and speaks to the villagers, and the
audience, punctuating his speech with rolls on the drums. Meanwhile strings of lanterns are taken from the cart and hung about
the yard.*

PETER: Gather round, friends all, gather round, Divine
Providence, ever on the lookout for sins to punish and
virtue to reward, has smiled on you. What massive good
deeds you have done, what charity, humility, love and
compassion you have shown to your fellow creatures, is
none of my business. Heaven knows what it's up to. Enough
to say that Peter the Puppet-master, the bringer of joy,
jollity and improvement of the mind, tearing himself
forcibly from the Court of Portugal in spite of the tears of
the Queen and the offer of untold gold by the King, and on
his way to fall into the arms of the court of Spain where he
expects a knighthood – is sent as a reward for your virtue,

to rest one night in your midst. Where he will presently present for your entertainment, your education and the good of your souls a new and hitherto unperformed history.

The MUSICIANS *play again.* PETER *immediately puts off the showman and becomes surly and business-like.*

BOY: Shall I take the hat round now?

PETER: Afterwards, dolt.

He cuffs him.

Get that stage ready.

(*To villagers.*) Leave off tormenting the bear. Tormenting the bear costs half a real a go.

The PRIEST *and* NICHOLAS *disguised, enter.*

PRIEST: That he can be taken in by you *proves* he's mad. Can you not be a little more ladylike?

NICHOLAS: You should have been the Princess and me the Squire, I'm no good at this caper.

PRIEST: I told you, it's against my calling.

NICHOLAS: I'm sweating like a pig under this lot. I just wish he'd stop asking me what this giant's like. I've invented a good half-dozen so far, and all different.

PRIEST: Well, our bird's nearly in the snare.

NICHOLAS: So long as Sancho doesn't catch on.

PRIEST: He daren't let himself. He's too fond of the idea of his Isle.

NICHOLAS: All the same, he's been giving me some very off looks. I don't know if it's suspicion or lust —

The PRIEST *crosses himself. The* INNKEEPER *comes out of the Inn, beating* MARIA *before him with a dishcloth.*

INNKEEPER: Slut! Good-for-nothing! Oh! you're back again. Just giving her a dusting over. If I don't do it regular she slips into a trance. Caught your lunatic?

PRIEST: We've persuaded our unfortunate friend to come back with us. Have you finished that item of carpentry I asked for?

INNKEEPER: That's all ready.

NICHOLAS: And we can rely on your discretion?

INNKEEPER: Don't worry about that, Master Barber – I mean, Princess. (*His wife nudges him.*) Mind you, this is all going to put me to a good deal of inconvenience.

PRIEST: You'll be paid for your trouble.

WIFE: The clothes.

INNKEEPER: . . . Yes, and wear and tear on my wife's clothes.

WIFE: The oxtail.

INNKEEPER: And the oxtail.

PRIEST: What about it?

INNKEEPER: We keep that to hang out combs on. Very inconvenient having nothing to hang your combs on.

PRIEST: I tell you you'll be reimbursed.

INNKEEPER: Ah . . .

The WIFE *turns to* MARIA *and slaps her with her dishcloth.*

WIFE: Get about your business then!

She and MARIA *leave.*

PRIEST: And remember – he may be mad, but he's still a gentleman. So treat him accordingly.

NICHOLAS: As for the fat one, you can do what you like with him.

The PRIEST, *the* INNKEEPER *and* NICHOLAS *go into the Inn.* DON QUIXOTE *and* SANCHO *enter the yard.*

SANCHO: We're back at that plaguey inn!

DON QUIXOTE: The enchanted castle, you mean.

SANCHO: Whatever it is there's something funny about it, when I keep landing up in the last place I want to be.

DON QUIXOTE: Fate draws us here. It happens often in the chilvaries.

SANCHO: Then I wish Fate would mind its own business.

DON QUIXOTE: If the Princess has led us here, it could be that this enchanted spot is the very place where the giant will manifest himself. (DON QUIXOTE *begins to move in.*)

SANCHO: Before we go in, your honour – there's a bit more discussing I'd like to get done. I'd like to ask your opinion on this Princess. Speaking as a Knight, would you say she was bechanted?

DON QUIXOTE: Ah. Have you noticed things too?

SANCHO: I've noticed things. As to whether they're the same things you've noticed, we might compare notes on that. One thing's for sure: she's a Princess by fits and starts. One minute she rides side-saddle, the next its straddle-saddle, one minute she's a woman talking, the next she's a man...

DON QUIXOTE: True, Sancho, I noticed this. My opinion is, she has indeed been enchanted, but only in parts and badly, perhaps by an unskilled wizard or an apprentice wizard, so that the enchantment comes and goes.

SANCHO: That's logical. There's nothing like an apprentice for botching a job up. As for her Squire, I know for a fact he's bechanted in parts.

DON QUIXOTE: How do you know this?

SANCHO: Well, his beard is. Else how could it be off one minute and on the next?

DON QUIXOTE: What do you mean?

SANCHO: His back was turned to me, but I saw his beard chant itself on to the ground, and I saw him pick it up and chant it back on, call me a liar if you like.

DON QUIXOTE: Wondrous strange.

SANCHO: I think so too. And here's something else: what kind of a bechantment is it when sometimes I look at this Princess Micamica and think I see that face-butcher from our village?

DON QUIXOTE: Sancho, I will not have you mock the Princess!

SANCHO: I'm only saying what I see. Haven't you noticed? Why she could be that villain's sister.

DON QUIXOTE: Enough, I say! (*He draws his sword.*)

SANCHO: All right, I'm wrong. They're not as like as two peas. I'm mad.

> The CARRIER *appears. He stops on seeing them.*

CARRIER: So it's you again. Come for some more blanket, have you? (*He goes.*)

SANCHO: Put my mind at rest. Is that villain a Knight?

DON QUIXOTE: A villainous Knight as you say. The same that touched my armour.

SANCHO: Then I hope you bear that in mind next time you see him with a blanket in his hand, and leave the ants to their own affairs. Sir Castilian! Innkeeper! Catfish-monger!

> The INNKEEPER *comes out, followed by the* PRIEST. SANCHO *takes refuge behind* DON QUIXOTE.

INNKEEPER: What! Are these your lunatics? I'm not having them in my establishment! They still owe me for last time!

PRIEST: I'll pay you what they owe you.

INNKEEPER: Plus any damage they cause?

PRIEST: I told you, I'll pay everything.

INNKEEPER: Well in, that case ... Welcome back, gentlemen! A second visit means a satisfied customer, that's my motto,

Let me take your – horse, Sir Knight. I'll get the beauteous
Dona whatsername to attend you. Maria! Come here, you
slut! I've a choice meal ready for you. Salt cod stewed in the
fashion of the district.

SANCHO: I know that fashion.

DON QUIXOTE: No food, Sir Castellan, for I have vowed
not to eat. But I would sleep now, for tomorrow I match
my strength against the greatest giant in Christendom.

INNKEEPER: Maria!

    MARIA *comes out of the Inn.*

Show the giant-killer where he sleeps.

DON QUIXOTE: On your guard, Sancho – there is enchantment everywhere.

INNKEEPER (*quietly to* MARIA): Lock his door. I won't want
any trouble this time.

    MARIA *goes in, followed by* DON QUIXOTE.

I can show you that bit of carpentry now.

PRIEST: If you please.

    The INNKEEPER *leads* ROZINANTE *away, followed by the*
PRIEST. SANCHO *watches them go suspiciously. The stage is
almost empty. Master Peter is behind his stage.*

SANCHO: Something smells; not fish, I know fish. Bechantment? Or skulduggery? I wish I was in my Isle now . . .

    *There is a noise from the stage. He whips round suddenly
thinking someone is behind him.*

I'm uneasy . . . There's a saying: an honest man has naught
to fear . . . Are you an honest man, Sancho? Well, I'm a
poor one. Which means either I'm honest, or I'm not much
good at being dishonest. A rogue should be rich, or there's
no point in it . . . And there's your trouble, Sancho Panza,
in a nutshell. If you were only a thorough rogue you'd be

a king now, or at least a merchant, and spit in anyone's eye. And if you were only an honest man, you might have nothing for dinner but you'd have the Kingdom of Heaven for afters, and spit in their eye again. But you're not one or the other, you're honest by parts and a rogue by parts, no dinner in this world and nothing to follow in the next. You're like one of those creatures the travellers talk about, head of an ass and horns of a goat and behind of a hyena. With a ring through your nose, to be led through the market place and made mock of. That's what you were born to and that's the way it'll always be. You govern an Isle? Fool! Idiot! Stop dreaming and go back to your village, where they're as stupid as you are ... Oh, I'm melancholy; I've lived too long with Don Quixote ...

NICHOLAS, *disguised, appears, pursued by the* CARRIER.

NICHOLAS: Take your hands off me, you oaf!

The CARRIER *grabs* NICHOLAS.

CARRIER: Just one kiss, my dear, and I'll give you a present.

NICHOLAS *fetches the* CARRIER *an unladylike swipe.*

Oh, a vixen. I'll fix you. (*He draws back his fist.*)

NICHOLAS: Hold! A word in your ear. (*He whispers, with much indication of* SANCHO. *The* CARRIER *chortles and awaits events.*)

NICHOLAS *straightens his wig.*

SANCHO: That was a pretty good back-hander for a Princess.

NICHOLAS: You there! Fellow!

SANCHO: That 'fellow' rings a bell. Who says 'fellow' like that?

NICHOLAS: Approach, I would speak with you. But not too close, for you stink somewhat.

SANCHO: If I stink, Princess, it's of Sancho Panza I stink, and

you'll have to take me as you find me or leave me alone, for
I can't change my nature.

NICHOLAS: It's not your nature needs changing so much as
your socks – but let that be; kneel.

SANCHO: What for?

NICHOLAS: Because I say so, varlet. Am I to call Don
Quixote to teach you respect?

    SANCHO *kneels. Meanwhile more people appear. The*
CARRIER *lets them into the secret.*

Closer.

    SANCHO *comes closer.*

NICHOLAS: Kiss my feet.

    SANCHO *looks up in bewilderment.*

Kiss – my – *feet.*

SANCHO: Is this a custom?

NICHOLAS: Haven't you seen this done at Court?

SANCHO: I haven't been a great deal at Court, Princess.

NICHOLAS: Then take my word for it. Kiss.

SANCHO: If it pleases you —

NICHOLAS: It does. Hugely.

SANCHO: Then it's no skin off my nose.

    SANCHO *kisses his feet. His audience watches in amusement.*

NICHOLAS: How shall I further humiliate him? Sancho
Panza, I'm told you'd govern an Isle.

SANCHO: I was thinking about it, Princess, if one comes my
way.

NICHOLAS: What are your qualifications?

SANCHO: I don't think I'd do worse at it than most.

NICHOLAS: That's an honest answer. Kiss my feet.

    SANCHO *does so.*

But you must know, unless you are an ignorant – cack –

brained – misbegotten – loutish – turd of a fellow – as you
may be for all I know – that honesty is not the first consideration when choosing a Governor. I must know now of your
lineage.

SANCHO: My what, Princess?

NICHOLAS: Kiss my feet.

   SANCHO *does so.*

Your lineage, fellow. Your ancestral line. What quarterings
are emblazoned on your escutcheon?

   SANCHO *looks at him blankly.*

Who was your father, dolt!

SANCHO: Oh, is that all? That's soon answered. My father
was a man of big affairs, and a traveller. Not to put too fine
a point on it, he only just squeezed in time to conceive me
between travels, and then was straight called away on
another business.

NICHOLAS: Do you mean you don't know who he was?

SANCHO: That's another way of putting it.

NICHOLAS: And you expect to govern an Isle with no father?

SANCHO: Not *no* father, Princess; there was a father there,
I'm sure of that, and at the very moment when he was most
needed; as for *who* he was, that can go to the devil; he did
nothing for me but bring me into the world, which I'm
in no mood to thank him for; so I don't need his help now.
In any case, I knew my mother, so I score one out of two
or fifty percentum, which is enough to pass any test. If not,
I'll throw in this: my mother, who told the truth as often as
she lied, swore to me that my father was in fact some noble
or Prince, on his way from one castle to another, who broke
his journey at our village – for some reason.

NICHOLAS: Then by rights you are a Prince already?

SANCHO: Madam, I only say what she told me; but if she didn't know, who did?

NICHOLAS: In that case a Princedom would be wasted on you. I'll keep the Isle for someone else. Go your way, Prince Sancho Panza.

SANCHO: No, wait. Mine's only a word-of-mouth Princeship; it doesn't carry Isles with it. What I need now is one on paper. They won't clash, I promise you.

NICHOLAS: I'll consider it. But only if you obey me in all things. Kiss my feet.

SANCHO does so. The BARBER *enters the yard, leading his ass on a string.*

Again.

SANCHO does so. The BARBER *stares at* SANCHO's *back, then at the pack-saddle and trappings* SANCHO *took from his ass.*

Again.

SANCHO does so. The BARBER *kicks* SANCHO. SANCHO *looks round with a cry.*

BARBER: Rogue! Thief! Highway robber!

SANCHO: Are you talking to me?

BARBER: I say goodday to you and you steal my property. I'll go to the devil before I'm civil to anyone again.

NICHOLAS: What? Has he stolen something?

SANCHO: You're mistaken, friend; I stole nothing of yours.

BARBER: Don't try and brazen it out with me, rogue! What's that?

SANCHO: That's a pack-saddle. Isn't that a pack-saddle, Princess?

NICHOLAS: It looks to me like a pack-saddle.

BARBER: That's *my* pack-saddle!

SANCHO: Put it on and see if it fits you.

G

BARBER: I mean my ass's.

SANCHO: By your leave, Princess, here's a mixed-up fellow; I'll try if I can straighten him out. Brother – for we're all brothers under Heaven – you were civil to me, so I'll be civil to you.

BARBER: By giving me back my property!

SANCHO: By ridding you of sin, brother, which is ten times better than property.

BARBER: *Me* of sin, you lousy knave —!

SANCHO: Of wrath, brother, one of the seven deadly ones. Watch this, Princess, and see if I'm not fit to govern an Isle.

He turns back to the BARBER *and tells off the points on his fingers. He is enjoying his audience.*

One: According to my master Don Quixote of La Mancha, that's no ass's pack-saddle but a charger's trappings, and if it's your word against his I'll take his since he pays me and you don't. But since the question is not the *thing* but the *stealing* of the thing, we'll let One go and go on to Two. *Two* —

BARBER: Rogue! Give me my property!

SANCHO: Hold your wrath, it'll be all gone in a minute. *Two*: As to 'stole' – I never *stole* your thing, to whit your ass's pack-saddle or charger's trappings, or I should say the thing of your ass or charger, if it *be* your ass or charger, which we've no proof of, have we, Princess? Let that go; I never *stole* the said thing, but *found* it, since to steal is to *take from*, which means you must have it to have it taken, which you didn't, having run off leaving the said thing on the highway or common ground where *I – found it –* or as it might be said, treasure trove!

He looks triumphantly at the PRINCESS, *who is rolling up.*
SANCHO *turns back to the* BARBER, *ticks off another finger and
opens his mouth, but forgets the number.*

NICHOLAS: Three...

SANCHO: I was going to say that. *Three*: Anything won in
battle is spoils of battle by the rules of chilvary; to run away
is to lose; ergo, you lost and Don Quixote won, and then
gave me that spoils, ergo it's mine. And if you've any com-
plaints about that you'd better see my Knight, it's nothing
to do with me.

BARBER: Villain! How can it be treasure trove *and* spoils of
battle!

SANCHO: I see you don't understand law, brother. That's
your alternate, your judical alternate – which means, if I
don't get it the one way I get it the other. But if it worries
you I'll let the treasure trove go hang itself and have it by
spoils only; so long as I have it, for I've got three ass-foals
to furnish. And now, brother, hasn't your wrath all fled
away, and don't you feel the better for it?

The BARBER *hits him.* SANCHO *yells. The* BARBER *grabs
the saddle;* SANCHO *also grabs it.*

Let go my spoils! Ungrate! Is this all the thanks I get for not
stealing your lousy ass as well as your lousy saddle!

*There is a sudden commotion within the Inn – bangs, crashes,
and* DON QUIXOTE's *voice raised in anger.* SANCHO *and the*
BARBER *stop, still holding the saddle.*

BARBER: God in Heaven, what's that!

The INNKEEPER *comes out.*

INNKEEPER: Maria! Where's that slut! Maria!

The INNKEEPER *runs off in search of her. The* PRIEST
comes out of the Inn.

NICHOLAS: What the devil – (*He goes into the higher register.*) What the devil's going on?

PRIEST: It's Don Quixote. He's gone berserk in there. I fear he may do himself a damage.

NICHOLAS: Not only himself by the sound of it. Should we restrain him?

PRIEST: We can't. That girl's gone off somewhere with the key. And I've promised to pay for all damage.

BARBER: Is a lunatic in there?

NICHOLAS: Don't you know a Knight killing a giant when you hear one?

SANCHO: The giant! He's found him! Have my Isle ready, Princess, for when I bring out his head! Keep your lousy saddle, I'll have an Isleful of saddles!

SANCHO *runs into the Inn.* NICHOLAS *taps his head with one finger.*

BARBER: Is everyone mad here?

NICHOLAS: Only some of us.

NICHOLAS *lifts his wig to scratch his head. The* PRIEST *removes his beard to rub his chin. The* BARBER *looks at them in consternation.* NICHOLAS *and the* PRIEST *return to normal.* Something wrong, friend?

BARBER: I think I've got a touch of Barber's Fever.

PRIEST: Nicholas, I think the time has come to secure our Knight.

NICHOLAS: Agreed. The joke's gone on long enough.

NICHOLAS: And reverend – when you get Sancho home, give him some penances; throw the book at him.

PRIEST: God have mercy on my purse, listen to that damage!

BARBER: Your name's *Nicholas*?

NICHOLAS: Nico – *la.*

BARBER: I'm hearing things now . . .

PETER: Right, I'm ready. (*To the* BOY.) Go on then!

The BOY *begins to talk in front of the stage, in a fast expressionless gabble.*

BOY: We present the lately discovered history, true in every respect, concerning the strange and ingenious adventures of the valiant Knight Don Quixote of La Mancha! (Spanish pronunciation.)

PRIEST: What?

NICHOLAS: Who?

The BOY *continues, telling the story and indicating the characters, as they appear, but without looking at the stage. He continues throughout the following, drowned every now and then by what goes on around him.*

MARIA *enters, running, the key in her hand pursued by the* INNKEEPER, *clouting her with his dishcloth. The* CARRIER *follows.*

MARIA: We were only having a rest in the barn. Ow!

INNKEEPER: Trollop! I'll give you rest! Unlock that door!

CARRIER: Come back with my girl!

The three of them disappear into the Inn.

BARBER: I've had enough of this. I'll take my property and go.

He begins to saddle his ass. The OFFICER *of the Holy Brotherhood enters the yard. He is leading by a rope* 1ST BANDIT, *who is tied by a rope to the* 2ND BANDIT, *who is tied by a rope to* SANCHO's *ass.*

OFFICER: God protect all here! With my help, of course.

NICHOLAS: It's the Holy Brotherhood!

OFFICER: Is there trouble within, Madam?

NICHOLAS: No – no, no trouble.

OFFICER: A pity. My duty is the preservation of law and the protection of rich and poor – especially rich. And like any honest workman, I enjoy my work.

See, here are two bandits I caught before breakfast. After supper I shall have them shot to death with arrows.

A disturbance within. I shall investigate.

He ties his rope to a post. NICHOLAS *and the* PRIEST *look at one another in consternation.* SANCHO *runs out, colliding with the* OFFICER *as he is about to go in.*

SANCHO: He's done it! He's dead! You should see the blood! He'll be bringing his head out any minute!

OFFICER: Head? Blood? Hold within, in the name of the Holy Brotherhood!

The OFFICER *makes for the door again, and is again knocked aside as the* CARRIER, *the* INNKEEPER *and* MARIA *tumble out.*

INNKEEPER: Help! Murder!

DON QUIXOTE *follows them. His eyes are closed and he is slashing in all directions with his sword, crying out the while.*

DON QUIXOTE: Hold, misbegotten creature! Your deadly powers shall avail you naught!

MARIA *runs to the trough for a bucket of water.*

SANCHO: Stop, Master! What are you doing? You've killed him already in there. Come and see the blood!

INNKEEPER: Blood, you crackbrain! That's wine! He's hacked my wineskins to pieces! Villains, Villains . . .

He pummels SANCHO, *then stops and cries with exasperation.* SANCHO *looks at him, bemused.* DON QUIXOTE *stops suddenly.*

DON QUIXOTE: Wine . . . ?

BOY: Now see where Don Quixote having quite taken leave of his senses comes back to the inn which he takes to be an enchanted castle and see now where he goes looking for the

giant and see now where taking the wineskins for giants, he
flails about and hacks them all to pieces and thinks the wine
that runs out is giants' blood, see now where —

DON QUIXOTE: Lies!

The BOY *stops.*

Enchantment! Demons! Lies! Lies! Lies!

He falls on the stage. PETER *comes out from behind it, pursued
by* DON QUIXOTE.

PETER: Get him off, someone!

MARIA *goes up to* DON QUIXOTE *and throws a bucket of
water over him.* DON QUIXOTE *stops shouting and fighting the
air, and stands still.*

DON QUIXOTE: Where am I?

SANCHO: Oh, Master, you've done it now . . .

SANCHO *goes into the Inn.*

PETER: Arrest him! Why doesn't someone arrest him!

BARBER: My basin!

He jumps at DON QUIXOTE *and tries to snatch the basin.*
DON QUIXOTE *too close to use his sword, grapples with
him.*

DON QUIXOTE: Touch not my helmet, scurvy Knight!

INNKEEPER: Take his sword!

OFFICER: Desist, in the name of the Holy Brotherhood!

BARBER: Not till I get my basin back!

OFFICER: Desist, I say!

The OFFICER *brings his staff down on* DON QUIXOTE's
head.

BARBER: Don't hit him on the basin!

The BARBER *tries to wrench the staff from the* OFFICER.

OFFICER: Help! I am attacked!

DON QUIXOTE *who has lost his sword, joins in. The*

INNKEEPER *goes for* DON QUIXOTE. *There is a confused struggle between the four of them.*

PRIEST: The cage, Nicholas!

The PRIEST *and* NICHOLAS *go. The* TWO BANDITS *see their chance, and untie their rope from the post. They look around for something to steal; the only loose thing about being* MARIA, *they pick her up between them as best they can for their bound wrists, hoist her yelling on to the back of* SANCHO's *ass and begin to make off.*

CARRIER: Robbers! Put my trollop down!

The CARRIER *engages with them,* SANCHO *appears at the door of the Inn, shaking his head sadly.*

SANCHO: It is wine. I'm as mad as he is . . . (*He sees his ass.*) Dapple! My own dear ass!

SANCHO *runs to rescue Dapple, and gets caught up in the struggle.*

The two conflicts resolve themselves. DON QUIXOTE *lies unconscious; the* BARBER *has his basin, which he is examining sadly;* SANCHO *has his ass, which he is caressing; the* CARRIER *has* MARIA; *and the two* BANDITS *sit again fatalistically on the ground in a tangle of rope.*

OFFICER: In the name of the Holy Brotherhood, I arrest everyone!

The PRIEST *and* NICHOLAS *appear, trundling a cart on which has been constructed a rough cage of poles.*

Wait! One moment!

The OFFICER *brings out a parchment, which he proceeds to examine, looking closely at* DON QUIXOTE *between times.*

PRIEST: Come, Nicholas, there's no time to be lost.

He approaches the OFFICER.

A word with you, if you please.

OFFICER: Secure this man! This is the notorious highway robber Don Quixote! Tie him up, that I may execute him!

PRIEST: That's what I wanted to talk to you about.

The PRIEST *takes the* OFFICER *aside, and they engage in earnest conversation.*

NICHOLAS: Innkeeper – a word with you, if you please.

NICHOLAS *takes the* INNKEEPER *and the* CARRIER *aside, and they engage in earnest conversation.* SANCHO *looks up from Dapple at the two groups engrossed in their talk. He unties Dapple and begins to steal off with her.*

OFFICER: Steal not that ass!

SANCHO: You don't understand, your worship; this is my ass.

OFFICER: That you must prove to the Court.

SANCHO: Where is this Court? And how can I prove it?

OFFICER: I am the Court. As to how, that's your problem. I shall hear your application next week.

SANCHO: But I want my ass now! Is this justice!

OFFICER: Justice is for the next world, my friend. In this one you make do with the law. Leave the ass or it'll be the worse for you.

The OFFICER *returns to his discussion.*

It's most unusual. However, since he's a lunatic *and* well-connected . . .

PRIEST: Then you agree?

OFFICER: In this case I'll make an exception.

NICHOLAS: You, fellow! Sancho Panza!

SANCHO *looks across at him.*

Though Don Quixote hasn't yet killed my giant, I've decided to grant your request. I shall give you your Isle.

SANCHO *doesn't react.*

Do you hear what I say?

SANCHO: I hear.

NICHOLAS: Then why aren't you jumping for joy? It's what you wanted isn't it?

SANCHO: When I lived in my village, Princess, things were what they were. An ass was an ass, a windmill was a windmill, and a barber was a barber. Out in the world, it seems that's not so. Windmills are giants, pigs are princesses are pigs again, Knights are base men the minute they start beating me, so my noble master can't dirty his hands helping me out of it; monks are wizards and inns are castles and cleanshaven men wear beards and magic cures nearly kill you and your ass gets stolen from under you by thieves and then kept from you when you get it back, by the law. As for promises, I've been promised a lot lately, with nothing to show for it but kicks, thumps, blanket-rides and the odd bellyfull of rotten fish. I've been promised an Isle, and I've followed that promise like an ass follows a carrot, and it's never got any closer. Not to put too fine a point on it, I've served my master Don Quixote this far, and I think I've served him well and I'll carry on serving him till he tells me to stop, because I love him and because I was born to serve. And when he tells me black's white or red or sky-blue-pink I'll not contradict him since he's my master; up to a point. But what I believe and don't believe is my business. A Princess you may be, and I'm not saying you're not. Then again you may be a pig and you may be a pickled mackerel. As to this Isle, Princess, I'll believe it when I can see it – touch it – kick it – smell it – and eat it. Until then I pray to be excused from jumping for joy.

NICHOLAS: Well spoken, fellow! For that, you shall have

your wish. You *shall* see it, and eat it too if you like, as soon
as you please.

SANCHO: As soon as I please?

NICHOLAS: That's what I said.

SANCHO: Now.

NICHOLAS: Now?

SANCHO: Now.

NICHOLAS: Good. Put on this blindfold.

SANCHO: What for?

NICHOLAS: Do you want to see your Isle, or don't you?

SANCHO: I see my Isle by putting on a blindfold?

NICHOLAS: You put on a blindfold that you may be transported to your Isle.

SANCHO: How transported?

NICHOLAS: By magic, how else?

    SANCHO *looks at* NICHOLAS, *at the others. He gets no help
from any of them.*

SANCHO: What kind of magic?

NICHOLAS: Seek not to know the inner mysteries. Enough to
say, a kind of magic flight.

SANCHO: Flight?

NICHOLAS: As the birds.

SANCHO: I don't like the idea of that.

NICHOLAS: You can't fall as long as you keep the blindfold
on.

SANCHO: How long will it take?

NICHOLAS: Not so long you'll be bored – and not so short
you'll wish it longer.

SANCHO: And I'll see my Isle?

NICHOLAS: All shall be revealed unto you.

    SANCHO *hesitates.*

SANCHO: Give me the blindfold.

NICHOLAS puts the blindfold on him, signalling to the INN-KEEPER to bring a blanket. Meanwhile the PRIEST and the OFFICER have been tying DON QUIXOTE's hands and feet.

NICHOLAS: Sit on this.

SANCHO (*sitting on the blanket*): What's this?

NICHOLAS: A magic carpet.

SANCHO feels it.

SANCHO: It's thin for a carpet. Feels more like a —

NICHOLAS: Lightweight, for flying. Give yourself up to the spirits of the air. Are you ready?

This is more to the others than to SANCHO.

SANCHO: Just a minute! I know the smell of this! This is that —

NICHOLAS: Fly, Sancho!

They toss him in the blanket. Meanwhile the OFFICER and the PRIEST have lifted DON QUIXOTE into the cage, which they secure shut.

SANCHO is finally bumped to the ground.

(*in his normal voice, taking off his wig*) Behold your Isle!

SANCHO removes the blindfold. He looks about him slowly, at NICHOLAS, at the PRIEST who has taken off his beard, at DON QUIXOTE, who, now concious, sits in the corner of the cage, his wrists tied.

Citizens of this fair Isle – allow me to introduce you to your brave, noble, handsome, learned Governor, to whom all do obeisance – His Highness, Prince Sancho Panza.

INNKEEPER: What are your orders noble Prince? We want only to serve you.

NICHOLAS: Would you like us to kiss your feet like they do at Court?

CARRIER: Let's give him another ride on the magic carpet!

PRIEST: Enough, Nicholas.

NICHOLAS: Let's not waste our energy. Let this be a lesson to you, Sancho Panza, not to mock a craftsman when you're but a peasant.

PRIEST: Come, Nicholas, we'll sleep now. We've done our duty, and Don Quixote's safe at last. We'll start early in the morning for the village.

NICHOLAS: As you say, reverend. Good night, Prince Sancho. I wish you pleasant dreams of your Isle. (*He goes off laughing.*)

OFFICER: Innkeeper – has your barn a stout lock?

INNKEEPER: It has, to keep my guests from stealing my corn at night.

OFFICER: Then kindly see that my prisoners are secured within. I'll leave their execution till the morning; it'll give me an appetite for breakfast.

The INNKEEPER *leads the* TWO BANDITS *and Dapple to the barn.*

(*To the* PRIEST.) The keeping of the law and the upholding of righteousness is a grave burden; but it has its compensations. See, all is peace; order is restored. Pray for me tonight – people like me are becoming fewer.

The OFFICER *goes into the Inn. Only* SANCHO *and the* PRIEST *are left, and, of course,* DON QUIXOTE.

PRIEST: I trust you have learned from this, Sancho.

SANCHO: What ought I have learned, reverend?

PRIEST: That the cobbler should stick to his last, and not try for that which is above his station. That the poor man should seek his treasures in Heaven, and on earth accept humbly that which God is pleased to grant him.

SANCHO: What about the rich man?

PRIEST: He is not your concern. One more thing: I put you on your honour not to be so foolish as to try to release Senor Quixada.

SANCHO: Put me on what you like, reverend, but not on my honour. As you say, I'm a poor man, I don't have honour.

PRIEST: I warn you then – leave well alone!

The PRIEST *goes in.* SANCHO *continues to sit on the ground.*

DON QUIXOTE: Sancho . . .?

SANCHO *pretends not to notice.*

Sancho, I fear this enchantment has overcome me.

SANCHO: What enchantment's that, Master?

DON QUIXOTE: Why, this that has put me here. I thought after killing the giant my misfortunes had been at an end.

SANCHO: What giant's that, Master?

DON QUIXOTE: The giant I killed in there. Surely you saw it too, the head on the floor, the blood running like water.

SANCHO: Like wine, say like wine.

DON QUIXOTE: But even the most valiant Knight is powerless against such enchantment as this.

SANCHO *goes across to him.*

SANCHO: Shall I set you free?

DON QUIXOTE: Impossible, Sancho. See, I cannot even pull my hands apart, such is the spell they've put me under.

SANCHO: They've tied your hands. Shall I set you free? Tell me to, and I will, and the Priest can go to the devil; for I'm *your* man, till you set *me* free. Just tell me to.

DON QUIXOTE *shakes his head.*

Your honour – your giant was some wineskins hanging in the corner; your Princess was a barber, her Squire was a Priest, your castle-keeper was an inn-keeper and your be-chantment was a scurvy, rotten, lousy, stinking, piece of skulduggery dreamed up by a two-legged devil's turd. And your Lady Dulcinea's a —

DON QUIXOTE: What is she, Sancho?

SANCHO: Nothing. She's a lady.

He sighs and sits down, leaning against the cage.

DON QUIXOTE: Sancho . . .

SANCHO: What?

DON QUIXOTE: Is it possible I have been mistaken? That we are no more than creatures going about our business, ants on an ant-heap? Is there no enchantment, Sancho? No nobility? No virtue? Just the ant-heap?

SANCHO: Go to sleep.

Night has fallen. SANCHO *and* DON QUIXOTE *are silent. There is a burst of laughter from the Inn as the* INNKEEPER, *crossing the yard, opens the door and goes in.* DON QUIXOTE *begins to sing his song.*

SANCHO: For pity's sake, Master, don't sing, or you'll make me weep.

DON QUIXOTE *is silent.* SANCHO *stands up.*

Go to sleep. I'll keep watch.

He picks up the blanket left on the bench.

Here, wrap this round you.

He puts it over DON QUIXOTE *through the bars. An owl hoots. Silence.* SANCHO *suddenly turns and faces offstage.*

Who's there? I know you're there. Who is it?

A KNIGHT *appears, in full armour, as splendid as* DON QUIXOTE *is pitiful. His voice resounds inside the helmet.*

KNIGHT: Sancho Panza?

SANCHO: I may be and I may not. If you're a wizard you're wasting your time; there's no mischief left to do.

KNIGHT: Wake your master.

SANCHO: What do you want with him?

KNIGHT: Wake him.

SANCHO: Wake up, master. Here's something –. Here's . . . Wake up, master.

> DON QUIXOTE *stirs and sits up.*

KNIGHT: Are you the valiant Knight Don Quixote of La Mancha?

> DON QUIXOTE *looks at him, but says nothing.*

It is necessary that we do battle. Unto death.

> DON QUIXOTE *looks at* SANCHO *who shakes his head slowly.*

Release the gallant Knight.

> SANCHO *opens the cage, helps* DON QUIXOTE *out, and unties his hands.*

Come.

> *He motions* DON QUIXOTE *to follow him.*

SANCHO: Master . . .? Is it your fantasy? Or mine? Or . . .?

DON QUIXOTE: Wait for me here.

KNIGHT: Come.

> *He goes off with* DON QUIXOTE, SANCHO *walks up and down.*

SANCHO: It's none of my business . . . The devil take it . . .

> *He runs after them. A moment's silence, the sound of battle and silence again. Then* SANCHO *reappears, carrying* DON QUIXOTE.

Come on, my Knight; we're going home at last.

SCENE TWELVE

DON QUIXOTE's *house.* DON QUIXOTE *is lying on a made-up bed on the trestle table outside the house.* SANCHO *sits near by, the picture of despondency. The* NIECE *is bathing* DON QUIXOTE's *face. The* PRIEST *and* NICHOLAS *enter the Courtyard hurriedly. They speak in low tones, as in a sick-room.*

PRIEST: How is he?

NIECE: *(tearfully):* I don't know . .

NICHOLAS: *(by the bedside)* He doesn't look too good to me. I think last rites might be in order, reverend.

NIECE: Oh, no . . .

NICHOLAS: Better safe than sorry. Then I'll bleed him for luck.

PRIEST: Oh, I'm sure it hasn't come to that yet. Tell me, what happened?

The NIECE *points to* SANCHO.

NIECE: Ask him.

PRIEST: Sancho, I want the truth. What happened last night? The truth.

SANCHO: What's the difference? He's back, isn't he? Look at him . . .

PRIEST: Sancho . . .

SANCHO: Right. The truth. After you'd gone to bed a Knight

appeared, covered in shining armour from head to foot. Sancho Panza, he said, for he knew my name without me telling him – let free your master, for I must do battle with him. He took my Knight out on to the road and after a bit I couldn't bear to wait so I followed. And, there he was on a horse the size of a camel, with his armour so shining in the moonlight I couldn't look at it. Don Quixote of La Mancha! he cried with a voice like thunder, all the world has heard of you and your valiance, and in all the world only you are worth my challenge, and so I challenge you! And they charged one another, and you never saw such a charge. Nor did my Knight fall off on the way, but kept on full tilt at this knight till I lost my nerve and had to look the other way; and then there was a great crash and there was Don Quixote flat on his back with this Knight standing over him with his lance on his throat. Don Quixote! he cried, You have fought nobly. For that I spare your life; but only if you go back to where you came from for one year, for there's not room for two such Knights as us at the same time. And my master agreed, as you can see, since he let me carry him home and here he is, and there he lies, and can't get up or won't get up, I don't know which.

NICHOLAS: A likely tale.

PRIEST: I shall speak to you later, Sancho.

The HOUSEKEEPER *comes out of the house.*

HOUSEKEEPER: This is a bad business, reverend.

PRIEST: Very sad.

NICHOLAS: And there's the cause of it.

HOUSEKEEPER: After all the trouble you went to.

NICHOLAS: And the expense.

PRIEST: One asks no thanks for doing one's charitable duty,

It's just a pity our plan was spoilt for we'd have had him on his feet and at Mass by now, instead of like this. Well, well, well, we did our best, Nicholas; no man can do more.

NICHOLAS: That's true, reverend. We did our best.

PRIEST: Come, we'll leave him. We'll return later to see how he is and take confession.

NICHOLAS: If he's still with us.

The PRIEST *and* NICHOLAS *leave.*

HOUSEKEEPER: And you might go back to your wife where you belong, after all the damage you've done.

SANCHO *takes no notice. The* HOUSEKEEPER *goes inside. The* STUDENT *arrives.*

NIECE: Was there really a Knight?

SANCHO: I only said what I saw. You don't have to believe it.

NIECE: And my uncle fought well?

SANCHO: He always fought well.

NIECE: I'd like to have seen this knight.

STUDENT: You'd probably find him quite an ordinary fellow.

NIECE: A lot you know about it. (*She goes inside.*)

STUDENT: How is he?

SANCHO: He won't move; he won't eat; he won't talk.

STUDENT: Perhaps I should have stuck to my books after all.

SANCHO: What does that mean?

STUDENT: You wouldn't believe me if I told you.

SANCHO: Wait a minute . . . That voice . . .

The STUDENT *cups his hands to his mouth.*

STUDENT: Sancho Panza . . . .

SANCHO: You were the Knight.

The STUDENT *nods.*

Why?

STUDENT: I was afraid they'd humiliate him.

SANCHO: They'd have got him back home.

STUDENT: Yes, in a cage. So everyone could have said; There's Senor Quixada, the madman; he fought for what he believed in, so they put him in a cage . . . people don't belong in cages . . . I sold my books to hire that armour and the horse. I spent two weeks taking riding lessons. I didn't cut a bad figure. Did I? Well, you didn't know.

> SANCHO *shakes his head slowly*.

Not that it matters to us. You and me, Sancho, we can do without dignity and honour. But they're all he's got.

SANCHO: Wait a minute though . . . When you were that Knight, you didn't sta-sta-sta——

STUDENT: No. St – St – Strange, isn't it?

DON QUIXOTE: Dulcinea . . . Where is my Lady Dulcinea?

> SANCHO *looks at the* STUDENT, *who shakes his head*.

SANCHO: She'll be here, Master, I'm sure of it; she'll be here straight.

STUDENT: Senor – I'm told that was a rare battle you fought today.

DON QUIXOTE: It was; a rare battle; such as you'll not read about in your books, Master Student, for there are not the words to describe it. Tell him of it, Sancho.

SANCHO: I've told him, Master.

DON QUIXOTE: That was a noble Knight, and a valiant one. As to whether it were Sir Rinaldo of Montalvan or the Great Amadis of Gaul, I have not decided. One thing, however is certain.

SANCHO: What's that, Master.

DON QUIXOTE: He would not be alive today had I not taken pity on him.

SANCHO (*to the* STUDENT): He's getting better.

DON QUIXOTE: Have patience, Sancho; we have only a year to wait.

SANCHO: I'll try to be patient, your honour. Meanwhile, get some rest. For you'll need all your strength when this year's out.

He goes with the STUDENT *towards the side of the stage.*

STUDENT: When a man's only got the one possession, you can't take it away from him – not all at once.

They go.